FICTIONALLY NONFICTION

The Life I'd Never Admit Was Nonfiction

Wynn Thành Phi

authorHOUSE®

AuthorHouse™
1663 Liberty Drive
Bloomington, IN 47403
www.authorhouse.com
Phone: 833-262-8899

Published by AuthorHouse 01/17/2022

ISBN: 978-1-6655-4942-4 (sc)
ISBN: 978-1-6655-4943-1 (hc)
ISBN: 978-1-6655-4944-8 (e)

Library of Congress Control Number: 2022900958

Contents

Chapter 1

HALF-WRITING HALF-TRUTHS

"Wynn?"

I had zoned out again. Turning my ring on my finger at an aggressively fast rate. I was sitting on the couch, looking up to see her face.

"Have you had any suicidal thoughts recently?"

Just looking at her, her eyes were gentle. Something about those blue eyes made me feel like I was falling into a cloud, strong enough to catch me but fluffy enough to make me feel comfortable. Just looking into them and looking at her smile, it felt like I could touch the truth. Like making a new friend, there was a certain amount of innocence and purity to her. Curiously looking at me, trying her best to know what was going on in my head; because that was her job.

"Some." *Truth.*

"How bad are they? What do you do in those situations? Do you have a plan that you imagine in your head? Do you have anything you can do to prevent yourself from pulling through?"

"I haven't really had any recently." *Lie.*

"But of course, it depends. Sometimes it's worse than normal; it has its ups and downs." *Truth.*

She looks at me as I shake my leg up and down and squeeze my hands together while meticulously putting them between my crossed legs to hide it.

"When it is worse, what do you do to cope?"

I write.

Every word means something. That's always what I've always told myself. For me, writing means a lot. When I was a little kid, the only thing I was good at was English and writing. Standing in a family full of the traditional Asian standards, I was seen as lowly and the idiot for not being good at math and science. As a result, I often kept my mouth shut. But my mom knew. Something in her gut knew, that even though I wasn't good at math and science like my cousins or my sister; one day, writing would save my life. I never thought I would be writing this.

And she was right.

Chapter 2

TOMATO-COLORED, MONKEY-LIKE DEVIL

had gotten to know my mom for about nine months when I started to feel trapped. I wanted to break free. I wanted to break free from your lies. My mom was so self-satisfied, I didn't need her. If you can't tell, Queen wrote the anthem to my short life. To put it simply, I wanted to see the world for myself. Even if my mom wanted to keep holding on, I just couldn't take it anymore.

And I was born.

Ya, I guess I'm overreacting. To be completely honest, there is not much I remember from this day. Now that I think about it, there is nothing at all that I remember about it. The extent of my memories is from what my parents have told me about it.

I was born on August 8th, 2003. According to my mom, I looked like a ripe red tomato of a baby. I looked like I had been sunbathing in preparation to make myself look good for the world. According to my dad, I looked like his little monkey. It still stumps me on how to go from tomato to monkey without getting confused at how I could be both at the same time. How can you be a tomato and a monkey? I mean, tomatoes are red, shiny, and plump. A monkey is fuzzy, brown, and energetic. How do I put those two together?

Anyways, both of them loved me, but I was a baby that was hard to take care of. Sometimes I think both of my parents were wrong; I was born a natural born devil. I was red and energetically evil. To prove my point, one story that I always remember is whenever my parents would try to get me to sleep, and I would make it impossible for them to sit down. I would only fall asleep if they were standing and cradling me, and I would screech my little lungs out whenever they tried to cradle me while sitting. Also, I always refused to eat. I wouldn't swallow, and I was a baby that needed a lot of attention.

Even as a little kid, I had my form of rebellion, and I would never be tamed. You could probably say I have been rebellious since the day I was born, and I broke free from my mom's womb.

Chapter 3

THE R-WORD

My parents were in search of a school for my sister and I. My sister is two years older than me and got accepted to an amazing carefree school, Torch. When the time came for me to apply to a school, my parents decided to see if I could get into Torch because it would be easiest for my family to just drop us both off at the same school. I mean it is the least I could do; I had to at least give my parents 'convenience'. I mean I was a troublesome, monkey-tomato, and devilish baby they had to take care of.

My sister got in with open arms. Maybe no one else ever saw it, but in my eyes, she was always a child prodigy. I looked up to her, and Torch saw what a delight she was. She was a fast learner with a splendidly sassy personality that *everybody* loved. I mean *everybody*.

Everybody.

Don't get me wrong, I also fall into this category of 'everybody'; but when your sister is basically Torch's most model student that was in a majority of their photos, people start to question what happened to you. I oftentimes was compared to my sister, which was basically unfair because she was a super baby and I, well to put it lightly, just wasn't. People loved my sister and she was the apple that fell close to the tree; I was the dried up seed that was blown away by the wind and ended up far far far away from the tree.

My adolescent life was full of hardships because I was born a lot slower than kids my age. I walked later than most. I learned to speak later than most. I learned math and English later than most. And a lot more 'later than most'. Let's just say, I was mentally challenged as a child.

As much as I wish that I could say that me being slower than most was just a ruse to help me portray my rebellious self and not caring; that simply wasn't the case. The knowledge would just never stick. Both of my parents would cry over worrying about me. I was never really tested to see if I was mentally challenged or needed aids for any possible learning disabilities I could have had; my parents simply persisted in trying to help me despite what everyone else thought. My extended family seemed to assume that I would have to rely on someone for the rest of my life because I just wasn't 'smart enough'. I simply would just have to rely on my parents till they chose a good husband for me to then rely on. This was a future my parents refused to give into and wanted me to be able to defend myself.

I was always called stupid by everyone I knew and they were never afraid to tell me how stupid because they thought I was so stupid I wouldn't understand what they were saying; it's not as bad as it seems and to be fair, at the time 'everyone' only included my parents, my sister, and my extended family. To this day, my whole family has found the habit of calling each other stupid because we sometimes make really dumb mistakes. My family has changed the word from a term of frustration and a need to hurt someone to a term of normality and comedic relief.

Since my sister went into Torch with such bliss, how hard could it be for me to get in also? Well, apparently on the line between impossible and definitely. When my parents tried to see if I could get into Torch, they turned me away. "They thought you were retarded," at least that was what my parents told me they said. This broke my parents' hearts. They continued to work with me and never gave up on me, and eventually, when my time came when I actually needed to go to school on time, I was accepted.

To put this into perspective, Torch was a school that wasn't based on a grade point system, a school that had a barn with animals, and carefree children in their ideal own worlds. That same school that seemed like it would not be picky, turned me, a little 'sorta slow' girl, away because they saw me as as the r-word.

I guess I can't completely complain, they did end up accepting me in the end. Throughout this whole debacle, my parents still seemed to be able to stand putting up with my troubling self and pushed onwards to help me try to get my life in order. Gosh, even at this age I was causing problems for my parents even without trying to. I guess I really was simply born evil.

Chapter 4

DO YOU WANT TO BE FRIENDS?

SHE SAID YES! SHE SAID YES!
I CAN'T BELIEVE SHE SAID YES!

Considering my slow start, you can probably easily predict that I was categorized with the people that don't completely understand human interaction. I genuinely had no clue what friendship was, how to initiate it, or how to keep it going. It made no sense to me. But it seemed like a necessity for survival. I didn't have a best friend. I mean, since I didn't even have a best friend, how could I be expected to have any friends at all. That's illogical, but it seemed to be an expectation. That is honestly a lot of pressure for a kid.

Every day I would hear my sister sitting at the dinner table telling my parents about her friends and about school. I would sit there and dread the moment when my parents would ask me. I knew it was inevitable and happened every day, but still, little me always was caught off guard and would always worry about how to answer.

"So, my friend today told me about how her parents make her

lunch and she is so lucky because her parents don't make her eat SPAM ham sandwiches every day," my sister would go off. My parents would laugh and tell the usual story of how our uncle ate the same lunch for years at his work and he survived.

> Laugh. Laugh. Laugh.
> Pause.
> Then the inevitable.
> Heart rate increase.
> "Honey, how was your day?"
> Silence.
> "Ok."

Ok, fine. I always said the same answer, but that didn't matter. I would always worry and I would hear my heartbeat its way out of my chest and land on the table to simply say, "Ok".

I wasn't much of a talker. I wasn't really a talker at all. I actually wasn't much of anything. I just sat there. This continued for years. My parents never got the hint and never failed to ask, and my sister never failed to tell a SPAM ham complaint every day. And I would not survive forever at these dinners if I didn't find a friend soon.

I had been watching these two girls that seemed to be very close friends. An outside source could even say they were best friends. And little me figured *the best way to find a good best friend is to find someone who already has one and seems to be a good one because they have done it before.* Basically, I had found my target. To put this into perspective, those two little girls didn't know I existed, but either one of them seemed like they could become my best friend. The best friend that I could bring home stories to have something more to say than just 'ok'.

Now that I found the *perfect* best friend, how should I approach her to become my best friend? That was the question that popped up in my mind for a split second before I did the impulsive thing that only I would do as a socially awkward baby. I asked.

"Do you want to be my friend?"

9

I was at least smart enough to know not to say, "do you want to be my BEST friend?" because *that* would be social suicide and make me look like a creepy stalker. Of the two girls, one of the girls looked at me blankly, genuinely freaked out, and the other laughed for a bit. The girl that laughed took a moment to laugh at my weird self and then said sure.

She said YES!!!

Ok, fine. She said sure, but that was still big for me! I went home and told my parents I made a friend and her name was… let's say Nosyla.

Nosyla and I soon afterward became best friends and I would follow her everywhere. Now that I think about it, I sorta feel bad for pushing the other little girl out of the way and stealing Nosyla away from her. Whatever, I was sorta evil and ignorant, so during the time, I just didn't care. I was a little kid. I mean what little kid actually understands what other people feel.

Even though I finally had a best friend, I still didn't understand friendship and I was midst question number three: how to keep a friendship going. I went through every day trying my best to learn everything about human interaction through her. She taught me how to play board games, what usual kid-speak was about, and how to challenge myself to become something I never really understood: a normal kid.

Normal kids had sleepovers, played on trampolines, played on the monkey bars, climbed trees, climbed things without any safety harnesses, and in general did things that could most definitely have gotten them killed. I was never that kid. Yes, I was a sheltered little kid who was always watched over by my parents and was taught what was stupid and what wasn't; but I also gave in to my gut feeling and fear because I honestly knew that I didn't want to die. So whenever Nosyla would climb onto the monkey bars I would just sit and watch her play.

There was one day that Nosyla finally convinced me to challenge myself and gain that normal kid experience I was seeking. And I ended up going to the scariest thing to me, the monkey bars. It was time for me to face my fear of heights and just do it.

One arm in front of the other. Breathe. Don't look down. And push yourself. My inner thoughts would repeat over and over again. I started to go. Breathing and taking breaks throughout the individual bars; all while thinking about what the point of doing it was. It wasn't fun. Monkey bars were simply a ladder sideways that lifted you off the ground. Gravity clearly is there to keep you grounded, but for some reason swinging across a horizontal ladder just to spite gravity is fun. Ya, ok. Sure.

I finally made it to the other side, and Nosyla cheered for me and was so happy for me. She then got onto the monkey bars and showed me a trick she wanted me to try. She hoisted her little body up through one of the spaces between the bars and sat on top of the monkey bars. I watched as she did so with ease and then gracefully slide herself down to safety. Nosyla came down to the ground and told me to try it and that it shouldn't be hard if I can figure out how to go across the bars. I looked at her, trying to show her I could be a normal kid, and then squirmed towards the start of the monkey bars. I traveled to the middle and attempted to copy her actions.

"Oh no.
Help. Like seriously help me."

It was like a blur, but I ended up stuck. I was not sitting on top of the monkey bars. I was not having fun. And I definitely did not want to be a normal kid anymore.

I somehow got one of my legs stuck in the monkey bars and the other leg was just flailing around. Nosyla tried to talk me through how to get out or continue moving to do the trick, but I looked at her with terror in my eyes and told her, "No. I can't. Get me help." She ran to go get the teacher watching over recess that day and she dislodged me easily. It definitely didn't feel like it should have been that easy to get down, but it was one of the most traumatizing moments of my life. From then on, I simply followed Nosyla around and convinced myself that if she wants to play, she can do the higher up climbing, while I did the groundwork.

Chapter 5

HULK HAPPY

Hulk. The big reckless marvel character that promoted the color green in the world. The one that wasn't the brightest, but did get super scary because strength came to him easily whenever he got angry. If I'm correct, Hulk actually explains it this way, "the madder Hulk gets, the stronger Hulk gets". You know he's cool because he talks about himself in the third person. Anyways, why mention this big ape of a marvel character? Well, it is surprising but I've always thought of myself as an equal to the Hulk.

This was all derived from one situation and further continued to increase, similarly to Dr. Bruce Banner. If you don't know the backstory of the Hulk, you should really educate yourself! But for this situation, Dr. Bruce Banner was a soft-spoken scientist who dabbled in radiation, and through time with large amounts of gamma radiation exposure to him, he became the Hulk when his emotions were heightened.

The situation when I started to feel like I truly related to the Hulk was when I embraced my role in my sole friendship and felt proud to do the groundwork.

Nosyla was going through a phase where she loved the pull-up bar at recess. Since both of us were little tiny babies, neither of us could reach it without doing the weird *Emperor's New Groove* broken bridge scene sort-of-thing. Once in a while, we would slip if our shoes didn't hold well enough and then we would give up for the day or try to swing from the monkey bars to the pull-up bar. That always never works.

During one day that we couldn't find a way up, I refused to give up. I didn't want Nosyla to give up just because there was the obstacle of height. I decided to be a good best friend with the role of working the groundwork. I looked at her and said, "we are going to play on the pull-up bar today".

I bent over and told her to get on my shoulders. Keep in mind, I was a little baby who had never ever hoisted up another person off the ground before and decided to carry both my weight and Nosyla's weight just so she can play with the pull-up bar.

Let's just say I may have possibly underestimated my strength and Nosyla got to play with the pull-up bar that day and every day afterward. As days moved on, I started to do that for more people who wanted to play with the pull-up bar. I kept pushing my limits and trying to see how strong I truly was. I had always helped girls beforehand because I would rather not pick up a dude on my back or my shoulders who have a different thing in their area where the sun doesn't shine. But I finally helped a guy get to the pull-up bar. Of course with a guy, I had to find a different way to help him.

Let's say his name was Gilk. He was a little boy with an average build, but a lot heavier than Nosyla. To be fair, Nosyla was skinnier than most kids our age. I was innovative and I got onto my knees and let Gilk walk up my back. But when Gilk reached my shoulders, he still couldn't reach the pull-up bar. We were about to give up when I decided that 'no pain no gain' truly applied in this situation. So, I had to tell him to hold onto the sides of the pull-up bar to keep stable, while I slowly shifted from my knees to my feet, and pushed him up to reach pull up bar.

I *am* the Hulk. I *am* the amazing Hulk. And Hulk happy when Hulk can help friends.

Chapter 6

TORCH LIGHT

Giving me years of experience with playing Mancala, riding Tricycles, and years of Jump Rope for Heart; I had to leave Torch. It was an inevitable truth at some point; I mean especially because it only went through pre-k till 4th grade. But my departure happened before that 4th-grade marker.

I have so many scattered memories from Torch. It was the place where I met my very first friend, Nosyla. The place where I learned how freakishly strong I was. The place where I learned of my fear of heights. Some of the most impactful memories of Torch are jam-packed with carnivals, 4th-grade operas, Halloween parades, square dancing, and the best one of all, hootenannies. We had themed hootenannies and we would dress up for them. The themes were all over the place. They included Dr. Seuss and farm animals. We would go in and sing so many songs, but one that we all knew by heart and would always remember to this day was Torch Light:

> *Torch Light*
> *Glows with love in sight*
> *Children's faces bright*
> *Lit while learning and growing*
> *Hearts ablaze with joy*

Torch Light, alive in every girl and boy.

It is actually quite surprising how many songs little kids like us were able to memorize at our age. I loved it, and no one was ever put in the spotlight or anything of the sort; we were all equal. We were all singers. We were all actors. We were all Torch students.

This joy of being in my own personal kid paradise came to an end when my sister graduated from 4th grade at Torch. My sister needed to apply to a new school for 5th grade and I would still be at Torch for 3rd grade. She applied to many schools but ultimately ended up choosing Congressional School of Episcopalians. The school valued and viewed as its top priority the creation of an inclusive Episcopal community. It was time for my sister to move on with her life and learn the responsibilities of taking life into her hands.

Not for me! Ha! As if I would force myself to grow up faster than I had to! I was definitely staying till 4th grade, just like my sister; and I was going to take my sweet time.

Only I wasn't.

My parents pulled the old 'convenience' gag on me again. Ok, I get it! I was a pain, but that excuse for the 'convenience' trick won't work forever! I left Torch a year early, and never got to get the proper Torch graduation or their super cool 4th-grade letterman jackets.

I left to grow up.

My parents asked me if I would be okay switching schools to the Congressional School of Episcopalians, and, of course, I said my usual, "Ok". I left and had to say goodbye to my very first friend whom I had grown so fond of. That was genuinely the first time I started to understand the one human interaction I had not yet known, separation. Going separate ways, Nosyla and I had to say goodbye. She cried and I knew I should cry, but we both knew as unfair as it was, it couldn't have been helped.

Chapter 7

MRS. @SSH*LE

Leaving Torch was a strain on my little sing-song heart, but I did get over it quickly. See, this was the point in my life when I didn't know how to do many things, but the one thing I knew how to do was to adapt. I was changing to a completely different environment, where grades were a thing; and I had to use my VERY limited amount of knowledge on human interaction to find a brand new friend.

Before I could officially apply to the school, I came in while I was still in 3rd grade and shadowed some kids to get a feel of the environment. I mean the real purpose of the shadowing is for me to see if I do want to go to Congressional School, but my whole family already knew that I definitely was going there so I might as well start to get used to it. I walked in and found my buddies. I was paired with this girl; let's name her Dledee. Dledee was a sweet girl, but, like most kids our age, she shouldn't be responsible for another human being.

Nobody at 8 years of age wants to become responsible for another 8-year-old. Dledee clearly showed me this and didn't care enough to pretend to be nice to me. She wasn't mean, but she ignored my existence. I literally was her shadow and stuck to her in the dark. She acknowledged me once in a while to make sure I was still okay, but that was it. To be completely honest, that was fine with me. I needed the time to observe and compare my data from Congressional School's environment to Torch's environment.

"Dledum!"

Dledee had a best friend, and let's say her name was Dledum. They were inseparable and they seemed to murmur what they called 'tea'.

"OMG, you won't believe what I just found out!"

"OMG!"

whisper whisper whisper

I swear at some point they sounded like little birds tweeting, and the phrase 'Well, I heard from a little birdie that _____" started to make sense to me. They seemed excessively judgmental of everything and laughed at everything in a giggly manner like everything was a stupid joke. At some point, they talked about me and checked to see if I heard, and I just acted stupid. I don't need to make a fuss, they aren't worth my time. Of course, this was in lower school, so I guess this all made sense why they acted like such children. But because of all of this, I did start to notice the difference between Torch and Congressional School.

Of course, I was going to go to Congressional School anyways, so it didn't matter much. The first day of actual school was an interesting adventure. I don't remember much from it but I do remember that my teacher had an interesting name. I don't remember it completely, but I do remember my parents couldn't say her name properly because of their Vietnamese accents. And that's right, you guessed it. They always referred to her as Mrs. @ssh*le. My parents knew it was wrong but the first time they said it, it sort of stuck. It was a running joke in my family, and as a lower schooler I knew that calling someone Mrs. @ssh*le should not be funny, but it really was. Yes, it was evil, but still. To be honest, it sort of did make sense... She wasn't mean, she just had a strict personality for a 4th-grade teacher.

Chapter 8

OK

Have you ever wondered when depression starts? Have you ever wondered if you could get rid of it before it started? I may or may not have had that opportunity, either way, I am grateful for the journey.

During the years following my fateful day one in the world, you could basically call me Alice. I was Alice on my way to my wonderland. But before I could get there, I had to go through my dark hole. My dark hole is something that I can barely remember, I usually call it my blackout point.

My life before 5th grade is all a blur and I don't remember ANY of it. But you may be questioning, "But, you just splurged your memories of your childhood in the past 7 chapters. How can you say you don't remember?" Well, young grasshopper, 5th grade onward I started to have dreams/flashbacks of memory snippets. These dreams would come randomly and every single one came to me in dreams without a timestamp; I had to figure out the timing of every single one. I sometimes can't figure out the timing of the memory and I just leave it and simply know it happened. For example, the time that I lifted up Gilk in chapter 6; I have no idea how old I was, what grade we were in, and I used to not remember his name. All I could remember was what

I saw in the dream: the setting, the positioning of everything, the way all the voices sounded, and how my muscle's memory recalled how each contortion and flex led to the events that occurred. It was like my body remembered the memory more than my brain did. By being able to see the setting and the size of everyone, I knew that we were all still at Torch. For the longest time, I couldn't rack my head around Gilk's name; so I quickly found one of my old yearbooks from Torch and soon found him.

Sometimes, it makes me sad and frustrated that I can't remember much. When people say 'you never had a childhood' because I didn't jump on trampolines as a kid, I never went to a thing called 'Jumpstreet', and I have never broken a bone; I just think about how me 'never having a childhood' is literal, because I don't remember it.

I've always been frustrated about the fact that no matter what I do I can't remember. I talked to a friend recently, and she said that I probably blocked out those memories subconsciously because my subconscious wants to suppress a dark time in my life; also known as traces of child trauma and PTSD. And I only recently realized it **was** a dark time for me. I was in a state between depression and not. I was 'Ok' with everything. I had no opinion. I didn't want an opinion because I felt I wasn't worth a thought. I felt like a nothing. A corpse without a brain, a body that is at the disposal of other people's wants. Anytime anyone said anything 'Ok' was my consistent response.

"How's your day?"

"Ok."

"Wanna go play with your friends?"

"Ok."

"Wanna go home?"

"Ok."

"How do you feel?"

"Ok."

Thinking back on it now, I feel scared. It was such a dark point in my life, the middle of my dark hole to my Wonderland. I didn't even realize it. I felt neutral and numb. I didn't have a conscious, a rag doll being dragged on through life. A rag doll that couldn't figure out if it couldn't feel anything because its brain was slow at developing, or if it was simply because it was traumatized by the feeling that I wasn't good enough.

When I was younger, I had the cutest little pillows! Notice how I didn't say stuffed animals? Cause they weren't, or at least not all of them were. I had one big bunny stuffed animal, and it was the cutest and pinkest thing imaginable! I mean you'd touch it and you'd feel like you were hugging a cloud, the epitome of comfort and love embracing you; though ironically you were the one putting in all the effort to embrace it not the other way around. Then I had a few smaller long ordinary pillows with certain patterns for their covers that were handmade by my mom when I was little. It was crusty and not the newest thing you'd find, but it was comfort. It was my heart. In fact, they were my family. It sounds foolish, I know. But with the smallest mind, there layed the biggest imagination imaginable that subconsciously foreshadowed my future.

Each one of my pillows represented members of my family; the epitome of feeling comfort and safe when I rest in my innocent sweet slumber. Naturally, my mom was the bunny rabbit! She is the cutest person I know, large yet delicate. Something I felt I wanted to hug the most, the one person I wanted love from the most. The one person who I tried to hug but I never seemed to feel the feeling back. It was comfort enough for me to feel like I could be there with her... I mean with my bunny rabbit pink stuffed animal. I had a long pillow representing every family member of mine; from my mom, my dad, my sister, my nanny, and my two dogs. Every single person I loved, every single one lying with me as I rested in my most vulnerable; in a way, they watched over me and protected me. All because I felt like my real-life family wouldn't. It sounds foolish, I know. Just some childish ideals.

It was eons ago, but I can't remember the last time I actually slept with those pillows, my family. But today, I got up. I made my bed. I layed every single meaningful comfortable piece of raggedy, familiar piece of fabric on my bed. And slowly a tear rolled down my face as I realized that that foolish child, those foolish shenanigans, they were the one thing I held onto because I needed to at the time. It was the one thing I had, or I felt I actually had to hold me and protect me. It sounds foolish, I know.

The feeling of not being good enough for anyone that I felt was reinforced by family every time it saw them. A feeling that mainly made a difference on me because I believed I personally wasn't good enough for life, so much so that an opinion uttered from my mouth wasn't valued enough to even take up one millisecond of air. It didn't see a tomorrow.

I was ten at the time. Or was I eleven? How old was I on that fateful day when someone lent out a hand to catch me? One day, my mom sat me down and told me that she was worried about me. She didn't want me to be 'ok' with everything. I am important to this world and I am worth it. I deserve to be heard. And I cried.

At this time, I had no idea why I cried, I just knew my body reacted. A speech like that can't just flip a switch and make me aware of what I want; but it did start me on that journey to recovery from a dark place I didn't even know I was in.

After 5th grade and after that short talk with my mother, I started to come to a realization of what I wanted and needed and realized I didn't want to be numb anymore. I wanted to be someone. I deserve to be someone happy, outgoing, and worth it. I wanted to be like my sister: happy, loved, and seen as amazing. Through that, I may actually finally reach my Wonderland. I decided to strive for that and become my sister. I mean how hard can it be to become someone you're not?

Chapter 9

HARDEST FIRST BABY STEP

I want to be her. But what's the first step? What's the first step whenever you find an idol and you try to become them? Well, most people sit down and try to note down every single one of their moves and learn to mimic the behavior, so that was what I did.

Giggly. Well, this quality seems easy to copy, right? How hard is it to laugh at everything everyone says? Very hard. That's the answer. What my sister found was funny, I didn't find funny. Also, I have never been a big people person and if I suddenly start being giggly, people would not start liking me and think I'm kind; they would think I'm creepy. So maybe copying that is a no-go.

Hug everyone! Hugging is a simple action: a motion where you grasp a person's entity in your arms to show affection and to show comfort. It's quite simple, so maybe that is something I could start doing. But then again, in order to be able to do that, I have to be able to approach them and make sure it isn't weird to hug them. So maybe that isn't ideal.

Say hello to everyone! Again I run into the issue of, if I can't even approach a person, how can I expect myself to talk to them?! Ya, no.

Be smart! Hmm. Now, this is a goal I can possibly get behind. My sister is the smartest in her grade and everyone looks up to her and she makes friends easily while being smart. So, maybe if I become smart I can make friends. Or at least I can stop being told I'm less than. And I can stop telling myself I am less than. This was it. The key to my success to become my sister: Be Smart!

My sister had a quality to her that made her naturally really good at math, while I just wasn't. I loved English, but I wouldn't say I am the best or admired for it because I was quiet. My brain interpreted this information as *I must be good at math to be smart! Smart is liked!* So, I started working on math more. By 6th grade, all my grades and everything about me was average, however I managed to get ahead in my math classes because I would work super hard and make it seem like I knew what was going on. I mean 'fake it till you make it' right?

Well, I made it. By the end of 6th grade, my mom went in to see my math teacher ask for a special request to have me skip ahead in math, and go to a higher level of math compared to my peers. All I had to do was take a little test to prove I was capable of doing well if I skipped a class. Surprisingly enough, the hard work and the faking paid off, I did it. The next few years are a bit boring academically wise, because I just continued to 'make it' more than 'fake it', though that component was always there. Now the results of this experiment: was I liked more? Well, to put it frankly, people talked to me more and the faking gave me a false sense of confidence, but I wasn't sure what to be confident in. If I still don't know who I am or what I personally want outside of academics, *who* is even being confident? *Who am I?*

Chapter 10

HUMANLY BARE

What is the bare minimum that allows our humanity to evolve? The reality is that the humanly bare necessity is the ability to reproduce and the ability to provide for your offspring's success so they can repeat the same cycle. That seems pretty simple, but since when did the gender of your offspring matter in that process? Since when did a gender reveal mean more than the fact you created new life for you to love?

Historically, in asian countries, there is a preference for having sons over having daughters. Often having a daughter was a disgrace and the neglect towards them causes high mortality rates in female infants/children and sometimes infanticides occur. For years, the sons were allowed to get an education that females were derived from previously. In the past, that was the reasoning behind family's preferences in having sons who could hold their own and provide for their parents when they age. As times have progressed, females are able to have more rights similar to males, but some individual families still hold this preference. Maybe this has a partial sense of sexism playing into it, maybe not; from personal experience, I believe that there are still stereotypes that the male will provide for the family, the male will have more opportunities and seeing your offspring succeed is prideful, and that the male is just stronger in every aspect in comparison to the female. Subjection to this preferment, as a female offspring, takes an emotional toll.

My sister was born two years before me, and my parents were content with her. I mean she was so cute and fun-loving; and to put it lightly, she fit the stereotype of a fragile girl in my parent's eyes. My parents decided to have another kid and they were hoping to have a boy. But instead they got me, *a girl*. They never mentioned it, but I felt some despair from their results the second time around when they were trying to have a boy. A few years later, my mother and dad had been having some conversations and decided to bring it up for a vote.

"We have something serious to talk about," my mother started. My sister, my dad, and I looked at her in anticipation of the words that were about to roll off her tongue. "Your dad and I have been thinking about possibly trying to have another kid. But I don't want to make a decision without making sure that we all agree," my mom put the hypothetical out there and my sister and dad jumped in immediately. My sister excitedly exclaims, "Yes! Thành [me] is annoying, she doesn't play with me and she doesn't entertain me. I want another sibling that is more fun!". My dad chimes in, "Yes, I want a son. I want a boy to do things with!". They talked over each other like squirrels fighting over an acorn in the ground. *Radio silence from me.* My mom looked at my sister and my dad in their excited state and adjusted her attention to me. Intently looking at me she asks, "Do you want a little brother?".

"OF COURSE SHE DOES!" my dad and my sister state on my behalf. *Radio silence from me.* I recoiled in my own skin and avoided eye contact with anyone. My mom grabbed my arm and took me to another room and told my sister and dad to not disturb us.

Stumbling behind her, my little feet pattered with every step on the cold heartless tiles. My sweat acted like suction cups trying to get my feet to find some stability on the floor as I walked behind my mom. Her grip on my wrist was firm but light, she held onto me. She made sure not to hurt me by squeezing my arm too hard, but she also managed to hold on in a way where if I tried to run I wouldn't get very far. Next thing I knew my butt found its place in a lounge chair in the room. The room's pure white appearance was clean and presented a luxury that none of us could uphold as well as it. I felt a shiver run down my spine, the cold unforgiving thoughts bounced off the white walls back onto me. My mom grabbed both my hands in hers, and she told me to look at her. Her eyes were sincere, her demeanor comforting, and she was the only thing in there that actually felt stabilizing. "I want to know what you want, not what they want. They can want whatever they want, but you are just as important. So I want to know what you want. Do you want a little brother? Really, don't think about what the rest of us want," my mom's calming voice called me out but still comforted me. *Radio silence from me.* I tried to look away, I tried to coil back into my body, but a part of me kept still. I couldn't look away from my mom's sweet eyes. It was like she was hugging me with her eyes and I could feel her soul patting me on the back and telling me it will all be okay.

"No."

I wasn't much for words, and I wasn't the most literate person. I didn't want a little sibling, I didn't want to feel like I could be replaceable, and I didn't want to lose more of my parent's love. I also didn't want my mom to have to comply her body to my dad's and sister's needs. We already had so many problems with just two kids, what about three. I didn't want to be a burden upon my mom. Everyday I think my decision was derived from a place of selfishness.

"Ok, I understand. That is okay, honey. Really. I honestly didn't want to have another kid; but if you, your sister, and your dad want another kid then I wouldn't mind. But it's okay you said no and disagree with your dad and your sister. I won't tell them what you said. I'll tell them I decided I don't want to, so don't worry about them blaming you. It's okay. I love you, honey," the metaphorical hug from her eyes came to pass as she grabbed me in her actual arms. I started to feel my heart sink. I felt selfish and I felt like I regretted my decision already. My sister and my dad won't forgive me. And on a certain level, I know my mom won't either even if she says that she didn't want a son.

She helped me out of the chair and we walked towards the door to the room. I felt a sudden gust of cold air pass through my whole body and knew I couldn't brace myself for the consequences behind the door. But a part of me wanted to have blind hope in what my mom said: *It's okay.* My mom reached for the doorknob and opened the door. My sister and my dad were right up against the once closed door and looked intently at both of us. My mom pushed through them and continued to stride through proudly like nothing was wrong. I, on the other hand, tried to follow her and hold onto her but was held back. My sister and dad kept me trapped and instinctively knew that I had said 'no'.

"You said no, didn't you," my sister looked at me resentfully, "why did you do that? Who does that benefit? You're being selfish. I wanted a brother". My dad didn't say anything, he just looked at me disappointed. And I felt myself recoil into my body once again.

Time passed, and my childhood was shaped based on that one event. I felt my personal guilt for thinking that I made the wrong decision and felt I had failed my family. My childhood shaped me to adjust to my dad like I was his son I deprived him of. I would tag along with my dad and act tough. I formed a high tolerance for pain and I put in the work to do the hands-on menial work. I helped mow the lawn, I helped clean dishes, I cooked/baked, I raked up leaves, pulled weeds, repair car parts, I threw out trash, and I went around the house making sure to not leave anything out of place. If I did leave anything out of place, I'd get yelled at for doing it wrong; though I didn't have to do it in the first place.

I tried to make my endurance last as long as possible. My dad always wanted a sport driven son, who liked to mess around with things and had a boyish curiosity to do stupid, chaotic, and dangerous things like he did as a kid. So any time my dad suggested we do anything, I would blindly follow. I competitively swam as a kid and tried my best to perfect my form, my speed, my endurance, and forced every muscle in my body to be engaged. I did so to try to make him proud of me, and he was proud of me. And I felt like I was doing the right thing to make up for my mistake. I helped maintain the house like the 'male' of the household should. I would go out and pull weeds with my dad, help repair car parts, and I would wear unisex clothing that covered my whole body to make myself feel more like the son my dad wish he had. I continued to do so for years on end until I reached my teens, and it has shaped a majority of my personality today.

I remember one day when I was little, I walked in on my dad in the shower and looked at my dad and said, "I want to be a boy, I want to make you proud". And my dad simply laughed like I was joking and said, "Haha, you already are the perfect son, you're even better than a son. You are my strong son".

Chapter 11

DADDY'S LITTLE GIRL

'm not entirely sure why, but I feel like I'm losing my mind. Thinking back to it, not remembering anything from before fifth grade is something I want to open up and recall. But it's like my Pandora's box. Something I want to open up, but I don't know if that would be the best for me or others, and I don't know if I really want to know. With the few fragments of memories I have from before through dreams I recall, I remembered snippets and feel teased by the knowledge and recollection I just can't have. One memory, in particular, stood out to me. One memory I want and wish I didn't remember.

As a prepubescent child (I don't remember my age or what year), I was sleeping in my bed. I used to sleep with my sister when we were younger. She slept a ways away from me, and we both were sleeping soundly in what seemed like really early morning. I was half asleep and half awake when I heard my dad come into our room. In no way was this weird; my dad used to wake us up every morning. But with my eyes closed, I heard the bed creak as he crawled into bed with us. Feeling the shift in the weight of the mattress, he lightly and gently laid behind me and hugged me from behind around my thin waist.

It was a comforting and safe feeling to be in his arms really. I remember being a real daddy's girl because my sister *claimed* my mom. My sister would get upset any time my mom gave me attention, and in no way did I want to upset my older sister and worry my mom. I also felt like my dad needed someone since my sister barely spent time with him. As a result, I gravitated towards being with my dad the majority of the time.

We laid there for a bit, and I was still stuck between sleep and reality as I calmly listened to my sister snore in her obviously deep sleep. I wonder what she was dreaming about when my dad shifted his hand to touch the bare skin of my stomach under my shirt. Leaving his hands there for a bit, I felt my gut knot; but I kept my calm by listening to my sister's snoring. His fingertips on my skin, he slowly teased himself and slowly *'leveled up'* to his fingertips reaching under the hem of my absolutely useless training sports bra.

What was I thinking to think I needed to wear one cause I obviously did not have even partially developed breasts? In one quick full-of-power like movement, my dad's hands were on my bare chest underneath the training bra and underneath my shirt.

Still in between reality and sleep; words, screams, and noises just didn't come out of my throat. The gut feeling started to twist and churn my other organs as my heart reached out to my sister hoping she could continue to sleep peacefully. He started to grope the non-existent breasts of mine, I didn't know what to do but continued to focus on my sister's snoring.

Suddenly, he whispered from behind my ear, "Huh, they're still developing" in Vietnamese. My heart sunk to join my organs and guts in the twisted and churning feeling. I guess I *finally* reacted. And as a reflex to that comment, I squirmed uncomfortably to try to get him to see what he was doing; because I wanted to give him the benefit of the doubt. *Maybe he didn't know what he was doing. I didn't know what he was doing. He couldn't possibly be meaning to do anything not in my benefit. He is my dad.* My ultimate reaction was myself turning my body towards him, and his hands ended up on my back. He let out a small chuckle and whispered, "Haha, I'm glad you know how to protect yourself and avoid being touched. That's good, my strong little girl".

That's where the recollection ended. I used to not understand the significance, and didn't want to understand. Something in my gut felt wrong, something felt wronged, but I ignored it. *It was all in my head*, I'd tell myself. I was in his arms, he gave me a mama bear squeeze, and I felt safe again. I didn't think much into the memory till recently when I had an experience with sexual assault again. I also just realized after going through that memory again, I saw/recalled it from the perspective of a third person. I distanced myself from the incident, I distanced myself from that version of me. Now that I think about it every memory I recalled from before 5th grade I saw it from the perspective of a third person. Did I really hate myself or feel traumatized by every memory in my past so much my subconscious found it necessary for me to forget and distance myself from it all to protect myself?

Chapter 12

INFECTED

There's a certain level of purity and innocence to fifth graders. I walked in and sat down. Alone. This is my second year at Congressional School, and I had formed a little friend group. Sadly, I didn't have any classes with them and we weren't exactly the 'popular kids'. And as you probably guessed, I'm no mingler.

More specifically we were the odd ones out who still played tag at recess and still played sharks and minnows together; we called ourselves the *Infection group*. I have no idea why we needed a name, but it stuck. In fourth grade, I was one of the founding members of this group because I was new and I met two twin girls my age who were also new and looking for friends. Unlike the rest of the kids in my grade, we didn't mind hanging out with boys and girls. And we formed our own little group. Their imaginations overcame their sense of reality, and I came along for the ride. We got lost in the fantasy of fairies, *My Little Pony, Teen Titans*, cartoons, and so many things that I was deprived of in my childhood, but they had experienced wholeheartedly. Soon our group evolved and we came to a point where every single recess we would meet up and play sharks and minnows, infection, and other tag games.

That was the time of our lives. The highlight of every day and what made fifth grade so pure and innocent without worry. The time before life got infected by natural chaos again.

I was sitting in the science room waiting for class to start, when she walked in. It was the new girl: let's call her Erial. She was a clean slate, without being influenced by the people I was surrounded by in that room. The way she was walking seemed insecure, lacking confidence, and worrisome of the time to come. She didn't have any friends, I'm assuming. And I knew how that felt. This tall, thin brunette walked into the room not knowing where to sit. Just looking at her and observing her, I knew that this girl could use someone to change her life, and maybe she could change mine.

"Hey," I promptly got up and walked directly towards her to tell her hello.

All she needed was a friendly face, and immediately after that one hello, we became instant friends. We hung out together in all our overlapping classes] and soon she was welcomed into the *Infection Group.*

Life was blissful and almost ignorantly wise at the time. Do you ever think back in history and wonder how people could just ignore the oppressions and discriminations of the world and life seemed to have a certain amount of bliss for those who didn't have to worry? Don't get me wrong, it was bad. Mental health wasn't seen as existent, religion justified the discrimination and murder of those different than us, blind faith in those who led us directed us to the most destructive wars in our history, and even the founding documents of America are based on vague statements as to please the classism and sexism of our nation.

Mental health wasn't acknowledged as a big chronic defining toll for society and individuals until 1883. Mental health beforehand was treated as an attitude problem, an act of disobedience, and a rebellion; the solution was a physical or metaphorical slap in the face of get-it-together and shut-the-f*ck-up's. But today, mental health affects everyone. Almost everywhere you turn, someone is medicated for depression, anxiety, OCD, PTSD, etc. This popular awareness today of the importance of mental health is a very large positive to help aid in preventing the number of suicides and there is an overall understanding for those around us. We create a sense of empathy for those who go through more than we do or we can relate to those around us and not feel so alone in our innately competitive society. I think mental health awareness is so very great in terms of making sure our society continues to be aware and thrive to be more empathetic towards each other. We can form a sense of true community.

But I've always wondered, *if we didn't know depression or any other mental health syndromes existed, would we have to empathize with it? If we didn't categorize it or label it, what would be different? Is there a certain amount of positive to that ignorance?* These thoughts for me could just be coming from a place of my familial beliefs. My parents were brought up in a very traditional sense and understanding mental health is hard for them. They don't understand it. And when I used to believe in the same beliefs they did, I refused to believe in my condition. I refused to believe I was severely depressed. I was told to "just push through", "it's a phase", and "you're just being a teenager". I believed it. I had that ability to have ignorance because I felt I didn't have to face it. I felt like if I don't have to deal with something, then I shouldn't. But I was wrong. I got worse. My parents have a certain sense of bliss from their ignorance, they don't worry about mental health because they don't feel directly affected by it. But once you know, and you've experienced it; you can't have the liberty to just forget. You have to face it. But until then...

In 5th grade, the only thing I was worried about was tripping during recess and getting a bloodied knee. I had grown accustomed to this new environment; and without realizing it, I formed an escape there. I found a place I didn't have to worry about answering questions with 'ok'. A place where I didn't have to change who I was to be liked. Though my sister still cast a shadow on me, I had a clean slate where the sun shifted over just enough from my sister to both of us. A place where I felt like the sun finally was giving me a chance and casting our shadows only down to our own feet. I had my doubts and worries about being liked, but that thought seemed to vanish. It was like the only thing I needed was friends to make that worry go away. I stopped thinking about it. I subconsciously lost track of my worries and walked away from my shadows below my feet to a bright and sunny place.

And I felt like I could breathe.

Chapter 13

IN-CHOIR-ING

My mother never sang to me when I was a child. Only my dad did. Now, he was the talent.

My dad was always a nifty person. He grew up in a household full of kids, under the supervision of an unlikely pair of parents. My grandma, my dad's mom, grew up in a rich family and was known to attract the attention of many boys. Due to historical context, she had to marry; and that was the only option for her future. It was the only option for two reasons: women's rights only pertained that to be the only option, but also, she didn't want to work. She had many options to choose from, but she chose the poor boy. Was it out of love? Was it like Jasmine and Aladdin? A princess and a poor boy? No. She married a poor boy because he worked for everything he earned, though he lived a simple life. He was a hard worker and he didn't fuss. She married him because she knew he would do anything for her and he would provide for her without question; unlike any of the other boys, who were all wealthier and lazier. But he went to war and got sent to prison for a while, coming back a changed man. He realized he wanted to do good with his life, instead of only doing good for his wife. She was needy and nagging, but not for her family and her kids; nope, just for herself.

My dad grew up as someone who had the freedom of the world to do whatever he wanted. He lived in another world in Vietnam. He lived another life. He would roam the street with friends, get in fights on the street, play in cemeteries and in the streets, and he took care of his own. He would still have responsibilities though. He had to cook for his mother and his family, and he had to find ways to pick up the slack at home at times. He wasn't the brightest, so he would try to be resourceful to make up for it. Even when he got older and came to America.

When he came to America, he had to pick up odd jobs in order to get himself and his brothers through college. My grandparents had split up to different states and all their kids spread about a couple states. My dad headed to Texas. He had to pick up a few jobs such as being a tailor, a jewelry maker, and he even worked at Arby's. He used his creativity and his resourcefulness to his advantage from his old life, the one of childish antics.

He is now a dentist. He was never much of a father. When I was born, my dad left my mom at home to care for me with the nanny alone while he left to hang out with my uncles who were in town. He wasn't ideal, and he wasn't fatherly in the manner of caring for me; but he was a good singer. He sang to me when I was younger, and he taught me to love art. He taught me that creativity and resourcefulness create a powerful weapon against life. I was lucky enough to inherit those things from him.

"Hey, Wynn?"

I looked up in shock because I wasn't called out to much. Or ever.

"Hi, I know you play piano and you are good at it. I was wondering if you've ever given singing a go?" It was the teacher who taught anything musical in middle school.

I shook my head no. My parents brought me up on piano and violin. They believed it would help develop hand-eye coordination and other factual things about the benefit of piano. I started out with just violin, did both, and finally, just stuck with piano.

"How about this? I really want you to consider possibly trying to do choir? Give it a shot, and if it isn't your thing, we don't have to pursue it. Okay?"

I nodded.

I joined the choir, and I've been singing ever since. It was the first time that I have ever felt like my voice was activated. Though I was singing the words and feelings of others, it was the first time I could let something out of my vocal chords about feelings. I got my love from my childhood from my parents, and I got the words and feelings from others; but now I sing and speak my mind and my feelings using my creativity and resourcefulness.

Chapter 14

MAGICAL

We both came to Congressional School the same year, but we ran in entirely different circles. Not even, we revolved in close vicinity of entirely environmentally different planets in extremely distant galaxies. Not even a similar star could pass between us, the distance was immeasurable. Basically we never interacted. You didn't know I existed, or I don't think you did, but I knew who you were. I wasn't exactly well known, I wasn't well-liked, I was more of a carefree outcast. You were the exact opposite. You are loved, looked up to, and people had crushes on you. You were the type of person who people had crushes on.

Yes *that* person.

Clearly, I didn't get the hype. I must admit though that it'd be unfair of me to not state from an analytical standpoint that you do have features that could be considered in the attractive category, yet standing out at the exact same time. Skin tone a beautiful chestnut brown, with fair skin. Too fair to be allowed to be touched by others, because you hold yourself up above those around you with a confidence and charisma that knows no bounds. Dark, solid black hair swooped gracefully across your head like a swan's feathers when at rest. Body built like a twig, but I suppose that is attractive to many.

But to get to the real you, your eyes hold an honest soul. Similarly to a newborn infant, your eyes have a sense of hopefulness you view the world with, a positive light in the world of many. Your eyes revealing you to be someone who despises lies and despises a loss of control over your ability to be you. Someone who actually has a soul, but with a misdirection at times. Your smile, radiating a room when you walk in. Your smile's assistant, your laugh, is the purest laugh of all that is so very contagious. Everyone loved you, as a friend and otherwise. There wasn't a problem with that and I never really cared for any of these physical components to you. Other's clearly love you for those parts, but I never noticed it. I couldn't care less. To be honest, I had to actively look at a photo of you when describing your appearances. I never cared for your appearance, I solely admired your strength to be so uniquely you, while still fitting in to the crowd. I guess I honestly just never imagined that we'd reach the point that we have today. Like star-crossed friends destined to unite and form a bond unlike any other that I've ever had; *finally*, something interesting. Something new. Something exciting.

The first interaction we had wasn't even really our first interaction, but it was the first one of importance to me. You may think otherwise, but this is my story to tell, so *hush up* for once.

"Nadim? Why are you standing?"

Our 7th grade humanities teacher was one of the sweetest people I will ever remember from Congressional School and her class was one of the most enjoyable I've had my whole Congressional School experience. We coincidentally shared this class together along with a few others, but we interacted mostly in this one. At the time, Ahsie and I were best friends and inseparable, and my human interaction studies mostly were derived from her at the time, but you caught my attention.

"I needed to get up to concentrate better because your class exhilarates me so much. I had to stand up to truly delve into my full extent of how excited I am to learn in your

class," *a typical Nadim answer, one with charm and finesse
to allow you to get away with standing out.*
The cutest laughter from our teacher, "whatever works for you,
I guess".

I looked at you in pure curiosity of how on earth you got away
with it. And to my surprise, my gaze was met with a look right back
at me. What felt like ages of staring in each other's eyes, I felt an
overwhelming sense of unease. You had a certain level of confidence
to you that was overwhelming for me, and I felt overpowered in this
duel. I was outranked. My only intention was out of pure curiosity of
your character, yet I find myself in this game of war. In real time, a
second later, you *winked* at me.
You.
Fucking.
Winked.
How dare you?! Could you qualify that as a foul?! I call cheating!
Referee! Someone! Anyone! Disqualify him!! How was I supposed
to respond? My whole body responded and my face revealed an
expression of full confusion and fluster. My brain decided to buffer
amidst the confusion and my response was one of full shock in your
audacity. I felt my whole body slightly jerk backwards in absolute
astonishment, my startled mouth opened slightly letting out no
words, and my eyelids beat twice to make sure what I saw was real. It
was. You did indeed wink at me.
Giggle. You giggled at my response as kids do. I honestly wasn't sure
how I felt about your reaction. I was mostly confused, preoccupied,
and unaware of the proper response. I couldn't process it to come up
with a quick enough and normal response. I don't know if anyone
else noticed you giggle at my visceral reaction or even noticed the
interaction that just dazed me with horror; but I do know that I came
back to reality again and turned back to pay attention to the lesson.
Like tradition, you continued to stand up every class period.
Whenever you did, I would look up to notice the thing moving in
the corner of my eye. Acknowledging your movement, you'd respond

with a wink, blow a kiss, mouth 'I love you', or any other childish envisionment of affection. And every time, I'd respond the same. The same shock, horror, and astonishment at how you've decided to keep this up. You decided to keep up this engagement of interactions, while still mixing it up with different ways of expressing your 'love' of messing with me. I knew you were doing it to get a reaction out of me, and it had no real weight in actual emotional connection; but I couldn't help but go along with it. Partly because I still hadn't come up with a different possible reaction to such a flabbergasting interaction; but also, it was kind of funny on my end as well. To see you laugh, and to feel like I was causing it and sharing a moment with you for fun was appealing and entertaining to me.

"Hey, Wynn. Can you help me with something?" One fateful day in class, you decided to approach me.

"What do *you* want, Nadim?" I responded in a disdained voice. Our dynamic turned into one where my response would always be of judgement, because I honestly found it funny. That's just my sense of humor though, and somehow, I knew you understood.

"I just wanted to ask you to help me draw a straight line," an innocent smile peered upon your face like a puppy asking for a bone.

I raised an eyebrow, gave a sneering look, and let out the devilish remark, "How many times did you try to do it yourself?"

You opened your mouth. Let out a soundless gust, only to close abruptly once more. Radiating an energy of purely not wanting to reveal the true answer, but eventually relenting and letting me know, "that is besides the point…"

Laughter on both our ends. I grabbed the paper, a ruler, and my pencil in hand and drew a straight line for you down the center of the paper as you attempted to do so many times.

"Thank you!! You are the best, Wynn! Can you now help me cut on the line?" handing me scissors, you proceeded to prompt me to help you more.

42

"Nadim... I just drew a straight line on the paper, all *you* have to do is cut on that line... follow the line, it isn't that hard."
Laughter.

"No, Wynn, I can't do it... or I can't do it alone," you seemed to be hinting at something I hadn't quite caught onto yet, "you have to watch me do it, then I can."

"... I... I have to... I have to *watch* you? And then you can cut a straight line?? You do realize that makes no sense, right?"

"No, Wynn, it totally does! Really!! Believe me!!! You are magical! Watching me will magically make me be able to cut a straight line!"

Did you just say I'm magical? "... Nadim..."

"No. Wait. Hush. Shhh. Shush," interrupting the words from leaving my mouth, you hushed me up to prove your point.

Scissors in your hand, the gator chomped its way down the line, eating the graphite as it went on. Slicing straight through with ease, you made it all the way through the sheet of paper, cutting it clean in half.

"See!! I told you! You watching me is magical! See!" you exclaimed in excitement at your accomplishment, not sure whether the accomplishment of proving '*I'm Magical*' or that you managed to cut a straight line.

"You can't even say that I'm wrong. You can't. See, it just worked," you continued to gloat.

"... Ok, Nadim... you can't exactlyyyyy say that you proved your point without seeing the alternative..." I pointed out a solid point of rebuttal to continue the banter.

"Hush. Shhh. Shush," quickly you responded to try to leave the conversation with a bit of your dignity intact.

Laughter on my part.

"Ok, Wynn. Nice doing business with you and thank you for helping," you let out your hand to shake mine. A way to mark a business interaction had been finished.

I stared at you blankly. I didn't like humanly physical touch, it made me uncomfortable because it was a hurdle I had not yet stumbled over yet to know how to do without being uncomfortable. I don't know how to approach this hand... this hand that seemed so open to grasp mine in it, something so simple; yet my awkwardness felt extremely terrified at messing this up. *What if I mess this up... Just don't think about it. Just do it.*

I reached my hand out to meet yours and *thank god* I apparently had a good grip and handshake, because I was met with a comment from you saying, "You have a good grip and handshake, Wynn. Very professional. Of course, I wouldn't expect otherwise."

That's nice, I guess. With three shakes, the deal *should* have been set in stone. However, you held on. You. Held. On.

Calmly, I changed my gaze to your face, and noticed you change gears. Your attention had been redirected to your paper. You grabbed my pencil that was lying unused, and attempted to pretend that this was normal. Looking upon your work, you attempted to write with your non-dominant hand, as your right hand was now conjoined to mine. Sitting next to me, Erial and Ahsie were observing the things taking place. Feverishly, Erial immediately grabbed my hand and began to yank at it back and forth, in attempts to free it like a fish from your grasp. "Let go!!" she screamed. I looked at her and told her to calm down, and just let it be, because eventually you would let go, and you were just playing out a joke. I was willing to wait. However, I needed to get work done, and I knew that you wouldn't be able to get anything done either with your left hand writing.

I suggested a compromise, "Can we at least switch hands, so we can get our work done? You can keep holding on if you want, just at least let me get my work done."

The compromise was set, and we switched hands. We held hands for a long period of time, as we continued with our work, until you gave in. I didn't care much; but, clearly, it would start to get weird for you after a while if someone saw us holding hands.

"See? Problem solved," I turned to Erial to tell her there really as no concern or rush. You walked away, retreating back to your planet and galaxy, as I went back to mine.

P.S. Nadim ended up returning back to inform me that he had to start over on his sheet of paper so he re-drew the straight line and attempted to cut it; and he did, in fact, cut it crooked. Maybe I am *Magical.*

Chapter 15

AWKWEIRD

My sister was similar to a guinea pig to me for many things. Because I got to the classes she had already taken, I used her books and her notes. When she tried something, I would watch her experiences and see whether or not maybe I would like it. My sister and I are quite different in our skill sets and likings, so at times it wasn't that helpful. But knowing what my sister didn't like sometimes helped me discover what I did.

My sister never liked robotics, but my parents made her join. They thought that she would maybe like it and she should try. But my sister hated it. My sister is lacking in hand-coordination and spatial perception skills. These challenges caused her to struggle with robotics and grapple to enjoy the challenge and competition. After a year of doing robotics, she ended up quitting.

My mother has known me my whole life, and she has known my skills better than even I have known. At the time I was someone who was unaware of who I was, what I was good at, and what I enjoyed. And my mother saw through it all. Though she and my dad were wrong about my sister enjoying robotics, my mom took a wild swing of a bet and told me to join. She said that I was someone she knew to like mechanical things, logical things, perceptual things, the challenge, and my understanding of hand coordination and special recognition were much more adept in comparison to my sister. As a result she felt that I would probably enjoy it more than my sister did. I didn't care much. And I said, "Okay".

I have never been in robotics before, so it was kind of scary to step into it all. I was scared, but numb to it because I had blind hope that everything would be okay. I walked in and firstly noticed that at least I had a friend there: Erial. Erial was sitting there quietly and waved at me as I walked towards her.

"Hey!"

"Hey! I didn't know you were joining robotics."

"Yeah, my mom thought it would be a good idea for me to try it out because she thought that I would probably enjoy it. My sister did it the year before, but she didn't like it much. But my parents thought that maybe I should try it... I thought so too."

"Oh that's exciting. I wanted to join because it looks like fun and I realize I should probably start doing more things other than just class. I wanted to do a couple extra curriculars, and this was an option."

Though her reasons were different from mine, at least her reasons were more along the lines of something for her sake. I was doing it for my mother. Also for myself, but that sort of was the second reason not the first. *She* actually wanted something for her life.

While I was thinking this through, that was when I saw *her*.

A bubbly, energetic and overwhelming child skipping in on a rainbow. *Okay, not a rainbow; that's an exaggeration. But you get what I mean.* Her hair was a beautiful blonde, frizzy, and chaotic; *hmm... seemed to suit her.* Okay, a new person approaching. Analyze:

People will like her. It isn't hard to tell, her behavior is easy to be liked by others. She seems like someone who people would be annoyed by but be able to be popular. Firstly, for her looks: caucasion, petite, skinny, and blonde. And secondly, for her personality and her charm. She is a bubbly and positively seeming person, attracting others to want to play or hang out with her. Makes sense. She could be popular... but she's here. Why is she here? That is very telling also. Her bubbly personality may just be an exterior. Being here in robotics shows she likes building, and has a more tomboyish side that she wants to tap into. *A bubbly tomboy. Huh, interesting. Calls for further investigation.*

"HI HI HI HI HI HI" *Oh god no.*
"Hello!" Erial welcomed this stranger to talk to us and didn't seem overwhelmed like I was. She seemed more happy to meet someone so happy. I wasn't so easily fooled, "My name is Erial!"
Guess that's my cue, "My name is Wynn Thành Phi"
"Bailey! Bailey Haer! I'm new!" *Now this bubbly tomboy has a name.*

I was quiet so I didn't say much but it was an interesting start. She was bubbly and unceasingly happily giddy, or so it seemed. So, conclusion: someone who avoids confrontation of negative or internal bad. That has its perks and negatives because there is a lack of reflection upon oneself. But then again, she is a child. Maybe that's normal. But she seems to compensate for it in loads more than I've ever seen. I've never seen someone so *happy happy.*

"Hey could you reprogram this to this block of code instead followed by this?" She was smart though, very creative in going outside of the box to solve problems.
"Sure, but I don't think that will work." I was smart too but I think inside the box. I keep her grounded to understand that sometimes simple is better.
"Erial, can you please do this?" Erial did nothing.

Bailey Haer. A new specimen, but something I don't regret trying to learn about. She had a sense of childhood wonderment I lacked, and I know that people rub off on others. Maybe if I hang out with her enough, it will rub off on me. It will rub off on me. *A bubbly tomboy.*

*   *   *

Dear Bailey,

One of my close friends for the longest time…

It's been quite a ride hasn't it. We are seniors now, and we have been friends since we first met in that robotics room in 7th grade. You were new and I was not but I was in need of new. I needed my eyes to be opened to the life that I was living wrong. You did that for me.

We have not always been so close and we have our ups and downs because of our natures. We don't like to cling and we like our space as people, but we both do. We both understand. It is interesting actually. We call it a specific word though. Do you remember it?

Awkweird. (Awkward + weird)

We are, aren't we. What was made as a joke turned out to be the perfect word to describe us. Awkwardly we are a weird combination of friends and the most unlikely of friends, but we just work. We get along and we challenge each other to be more social, more crazy, more awkward, more weird, and more awkweird.

We don't always talk and we don't always work, but it never shatters our friendship. We don't talk for like 3 months on end and we can still hang out afterwards like nothing has changed. Our dynamic is one I would never rid myself of.

You are special to me. We all have our issues and we both do. Our own and ones together. But I accept you for yours. You accept me for mine ever since the very first day.

In 7th grade, we met in robotics and through Erial technically. But we bonded over our respect for each other in our common goal. Robotics and Erial allowed us to work together and understand each other to be able to do well in competition and in our partnership.

In 8th grade, we were kind of close, but we did distance. I was friends with several people and you were also, but we were general friends.

Freshman year, I disappeared. I focused myself and isolated myself in my academics and extracurriculars, so I rarely was around to hang out with you and our friends. But we did have our few moments where we would talk. I was around every morning before school, where we would hang out with the gang. We would laugh, talk, and you would mess with me as I tried to sleep.

Sophomore year, I was around more often, and we bonded. We bonded over more time just hanging out with each other. I wasn't tied up in as many extracurriculars, and I spent more time understanding who I was socially and emotionally. I didn't talk to you about my emotions and I didn't talk to you about personal private things, but we talked about drama. We talked about fun plans. We talked about ridiculous meaningless shit. Just teenager and childish shit.

Junior year, we didn't hang out much. You had a boyfriend and I wasn't in your boyfriend's friend group. I realized it was my turn to pay back and I would always be your friend. We've had our breaks, we would be okay. I wanted you to grow too. And you flew away like a butterfly and grew. I watched you fly away and your wings spread to show a beautiful design.

You broke up with him and you've had another relationship after that but now we hang out more. We are back to our hanging out period. And soon we will go off to college. But I know whenever we get back to town for holidays and other things, we will be back to our usual thing. Our awkweird thing. And I wouldn't change a thing.

Love you and Awkweird with you,

Wynn Thành Phi

Chapter 16

HOUSE FROM A HOME

People have different reasons for moving
Rich to Richer appeal,
Poor to Richer conceal,
Rich to Poor ordeal,
Poor to Poorer, my dear,
House to Home,
Home to House,
Welcome to the nature of moving

Welcome! Welcome!
Come in!
Step on into your new… home?
This house was built by a family
Family friendly
They loved it, yet they sold it
Want to buy it?

Welcome! Welcome!
Come in!
Step on into your new... home?
This is a good neighborhood!
Well lit
Guarantee satisfaction by the owners, yet they sold it
Want to buy it?

Welcome! Welcome!
Come in!
Step on into your new... home?
A modern home is what you seek?
Well you've found the right place!
Highly recommended by others, yet someone sold it
Want to buy it?

Welcome! Welcome!
Come in!
Step on into your new... land?
You may not be seeking a new home,
But this land is perfect for building a beautiful house
The land is perfect and very fertile
Want to buy?

Rich to Richer appeal was the dream
His and Hers
House from a home
Was what saw
Materialistic poison
Murdering the real feeling
Aimless zombies building
To gloat a newfound sense of pride
Pride
Making a home a house
A House from A Home

Bye to my home
Packing to a new reality
I know this is the start of the collapse
Building a building with your own hands
Only to watch the structure crumble by those same hands.
…
Want to buy?

Chapter 17

CANCEROUS

If not for traditions, where would we be culturally? Traditions shape our ways of life and allow us to have a connection to our culture and our families. I can't speak for predominantly caucasion families, but for my Vietnamese family we have many traditions we uphold. Some are more culturally captivating in terms of belief. We have alters and praise our ancestors and we have rituals we uphold on certain days of the year. We celebrate the Lunar New Year and other holidays. But a more unconventional tradition we upkeep is one we do every year... or we used to.

My family is Buddhist, but we have a couple extended family who have shifted to Christianity, an odd jump but one nonetheless. I am not one to judge on someone's beliefs, because our beliefs shape who we are and for me, my beliefs I can only hope benefit me in a way and theirs benefit them. No religion is prevailing over another, because each has granted the individual something different. Because of this, my family celebrates Christmas. We celebrate Christmas for the family members that are Christians and also to celebrate my Grandmother's birthday, which happens to be on Christmas Day. So it is a win for us all, because we come to visit her every year and we also get gifts too. It has been a tradition I've done since I was a baby.

We would drive to Austin for a couple days at my Grandmother's house and then we would stay till her birthday, leaving the day after. Each trip was different.

I wasn't the most social child, and so it was even difficult for me to hang out with my family. Families should be easier than people at school or people outside, but I still faced struggle. My sister was loved though, obviously. My sister was talkative, sassy, and she was a laugh for everyone. But behind closed doors, in our room, my sister would complain and speak negatively about it all. Rumors, that is what my sister loved. We would gossip about our relatives' private, social and family lives behind closed doors with our mother. My mom and my sister mostly gave the input while I sat and listened while playing phone games. I've never been a big fan of hearsay, but they made it so seemingly normal. I bet everyone else is doing this about us too.

I would mostly just sit in the room with my mom, and not leave unless my sister got mad at me for being so weirdly awkward and alone and dragged me out. But every time it would go the same way: she would pull me out, drag me to hang out with our cousins, and eventually they would all leave me to hang out in a different room, leaving me to roam around the house trying to not be as awkward as my sister already made me feel. Every year was a little different and I found a level of joy in different ways every year. There was always something or someone there who didn't make me feel so weird every year. Some years it was winning at badminton, others it was singing karaoke, and some was just hanging out with my little cousin to try to get her off of her device. I always tried to make it fun.

2018 was a little different though. My mom finally cracked. She broke. She got furiated by the nagging, making fun, poking, prodding, and devilish nature of my family and burst.

"You know I've had cancer for two years." *Shock.* That's all I could remember about what was on everyone's face simultaneously as our human minds processed. My dad was in front of his family and tried to act like he knew, but he didn't. None of us did. But it's all about appearances, right? That's why we talk behind closed doors. That's why my dad talked behind my mom's back to me and my sister about his frustration in her secret. That's why my sister did the same behind my mom and my dad's back to me. That's why mom hid it all. It all happens behind closed doors, because we can't be seen as anything less than the facade we try to uphold, while our souls are withering in the deceit. That's why, behind closed doors, I was simply worried if I would lose my mom and the rest of my family in the process of this domino that has toppled over. It was almost... cancerous.

Chapter 18

A NIGHTMARE

Most normal kids have nightmares about ghosts, vampires, clowns, and/or superficially 'scary' things. Ya, I'm *no* normal kid. I rarely dream; but when I do, I either dream about memories or I have this one recurring nightmare that seems to stay in my head like a broken record player mixed with hints of PTSD:

It's a normal school day. Walking the halls, I feel an eerie feeling the walls are caving in on themselves, in on me. But I continued to walk, I don't seem to be bothered by it. I barely even notice it. My body and mind were moving in a way all on their own. I didn't have a conscience, mostly blankly walking. Just there thoughtlessly. I didn't have enough control to truly question it in the dream. Instead, I just walked. It felt like there was no one else in the ghostly school. My view of the world dimmed down to a blurry path.

Walking onward, I reached a door frame. A white door frame, clean and crisp. Angular in a way with a direct answer. I passed it and felt the dark world be left behind the horizon of the door. I entered the class. This time it was my English class, my favorite. With every variation of the dream, that changes. And everyone ignored me, just how I liked it. I liked to be in silence and listen in on the conversations around me analyzing those around me more than I enjoyed participating in those conversations myself. In the far back corner, the chirping kids speaking of rumors and drama of another classmate who was not present. To my left, simultaneously I listened to these other kids discussing a conversation about the test to come. To my right, kids laughing at a meme. In the other far corner, kids talking about me, and how I speak like I'm presenting a marketing pitch. Everything said, it was all-important and this felt quite normal. I felt I was in my rightful place and the room was brightly lit. Surrounding me, white shelves holding books, a whiteboard, white tables, and white glaring through the windows from the radiation of the sun. Everything felt right. Clean. Uncomplicated.

My teacher walked in, and quickly all the students retracted back to their designated seats quickly like they were connected to the chairs by an elastic band. It was almost inhuman. My teacher simultaneously slowly walked to the center of the front of the class, starting her lesson. I wasn't really listening. I just wasn't entirely there.

Bvvvvvv! BVvVvvVV! BVVVVVVVVVVVVVV!!!

My phone began to ring, and I looked down at my table. Prior, there was nothing there, but my phone magically appeared directly below my face. The dark screen read, 'Mommy Phi is calling...' I felt myself get sucked into the darkness of the screen and get consumed by the words. My mom would never call me at school unless it was an emergency, I knew that. I looked up to a dimmer room, a spotlight on me and my phone.

"Excuse me, my mom is calling me. I think it is an emergency, do you mind if I walk into the hallway to answer it?" My comment was received with a brisk whisk of my teacher's hand and an understanding head nod. Grabbing the phone, I immediately answered while actively pursuing the door. Everyone was quiet and watching me leave. Back in the dark hallway, I took a seat against the wall, with my butt on the ground.

"Hello? Is something wrong?"

My voice was met with a stranger, "Excuse me, are you related to Hạnh Chau?"

"Yes? Who is this? And why do you have my mom's phone?"

"Your mom is in the hospital, you were under her emergency
contacts and she told me that you would be the one she
wanted me to contact about this."

My heart dropped. My breathing took a leap of faith to last over
five minutes. My eyes looked off into the distance but focused on
nothing. My head was terrified, upset, and worried. My heart climbed
up my rib cage ladder to my throat and banged at the roof of my
mouth. *OPEN! Say something! You know that in this case, you have to
be calm and go to her. Go To Her!*

"Where." my posture straightened and I knew what I had to do.

"Don't you want to know why she's in the hospital first?"

"No. Where."

"I am going to give the phone to your mother now," the voice
on the other end said in a way that I just knew my mom
gestured for the phone to stop me. She wasn't going to.

"Honey?" my mom's honey-sweet and graceful voice spoke
through the phone.

"Where Are You."

"No, stay at school, honey. I'm fine. Just stay at school."

"No. Where."

"...Honey..."

"Where."

My mom gave me the destination of the hospital, and I immediately
told her, "I'm coming. I don't care what you say, I'm coming. Please
wait for me. Fight for me. Wait. I'll be there soon." I hung up and ran
into the classroom. The room was no longer brightly lit, the room had
dimmed down to the same dark shade as the hallway. But I didn't
care. I needed to go see my mom.

"Is everything okay?" my teacher looked at me, I couldn't see her face anymore. It was too dark, and the fog covered her whole face.

Without looking at her, I responded briskly, "No. I have to go. I just… have to go."

Before my teacher could refute, I grabbed my bag and jolted out of the room. The minute I passed the once pure door frame, I was in the hospital room with my mom. The whole room was white with shades of cream and blues. I walked up to the hospital bed and looked at my mom.

"Honey." *she was in pain. She was leaving. I could just hear the guilt in her voice for leaving.*

"Don't feel guilty. Mommy, I love you. I always will and always have, but it's okay. I'll be okay. You can go. I know you are hurting, I know you are tired. It's okay. You know I love you and I forgive you," hand grasped in mine, I kissed her on the forehead and hugged her as I felt her life leave her body.

Startled, I wake up crying. Every time, I can't help but cry. I curl up in bed hugging my pillow, just wishing to never see that ever again. But I do. Over. And over. And over again. Throughout the rest of the day, just flashes of that image in the hospital. And again the next time I have a nightmare. I don't want to ever have her go through that again. Where she is alone in her pain, and she feels like she did something wrong. I don't want to lose her. Not like that. I don't want her to go. Please.

Mommy, please don't leave me. Please.

Chapter 19

CLEAN

"**M**ommy! Mommy! I got something in the mail!" *I never get anything in the mail, this is new and fun.* It came in a large packet and I was so excited to see what it was. It was addressed to *The Parents of Wynn Thành Phi*. I sat down with my mom (who knows where my dad was) and we opened the packet together.

Congratulations! Enclosed in the packet was an opportunity that changed my life forever. I was given a once-in-a-lifetime opportunity to attend the National Student Leadership Conference (NSLC). Each school around the world nominated a few students from their peers to be able to take this opportunity. I was lucky enough to be one of those students for my school. The way this worked, according to the pamphlet in the packet, was that I was able to choose out of a whole bunch of colleges and sessions that they were hosting in order to delve into my future. Each one was specified for each profession or interest. I had recently been talking to my mother about my future. Internally I never felt that I would make it to any future, and I have never felt any sense of hope or longing for anything for my future. Both my mother and I found that this opportunity would probably help me with that. After a long grueling couple hours, my mother and

I came to the conclusion that I wanted to attend the Bioengineering and Medicine and Healthcare sessions at UC Berkeley.

> "Honey, this is the first time you're going to be far away from home without me or anyone else around you... do you think you'll be okay?"
>
> "I'm a little scared. But I'm excited and I think that this will be good. I really think so," *I need a change. I need to get out of my head. And Congressional School just handed me the perfect opportunity to do so, and it was for me. This is for me. Not for anyone in my family, not for anyone else, just me.*

Though my mother was scared, she knew me well enough to know that I meant what I said. She trusted me enough to know how to handle myself and she also wanted me to grow. Though she had held sort of a harness around my neck for my whole life and held my hand aiding me by telling me what to do, she decided to let me do this. She believed I could take care of myself. For the first time, she let me go. She let me take the risk that changed my life. And it was well worth it.

At this conference, I felt a level of awakening and felt the real definition of a "clean-slate". I was in California and I felt, for once, at home. I had never felt this way before, but it was like a breath of fresh air. I was someone new, and people actually gravitated towards me instead of away. I was the person I never realized I could be. I was liked, wanted, and loved. It was like a dream. I knew at that moment, this was where I was meant to be. No lingering memories and no haunting thoughts could hold me back to my family any longer, I was home. I didn't even think about it. It was so blissful. It was as beachy and as peachy as it sounds. *California: eureka to such a clean start in a place I have felt like I've lived forever.*

Chapter 20

MORNING SHOWER

I picked up the article and I began to read.
She was so tired and so ready to crash land into the bed that was beautifully laid before her.

7 hours.

7 long grueling *hours* of being trapped in a hot car with her dad.

7 hours of his mood swings and babbling mouth.

Ugh. 7 hours of something she honestly already blurred out of her memory because all she could remember was an urge to jump out the car and become the roadkill she already felt like inside.

Dragging her own suitcase and her dad's upstairs, her dad stood downstairs with her uncle chatting up a storm, catching up. The last time she was there she was either too young to remember or she probably just blocked it out of her mind. That was also the last time her dad saw his brother. His brother who lived in California far away from the rest of the family. The brother that made it big and kicked out his own father out of his home because it was a 'money liability'. The brother that the little girl didn't remember, just knew him from stories.

Her dad left soon after to pick up her sister and a friend from the airport. Her sister just got back from a study abroad trip to Vietnam with a work group. They spent their time helping in hospitals and group bonding. She got a lot of friends on that trip and her sister never crossed her mind except for once, to get her a single blue bracelet with a pig pendant. Her dad left to go pick them up from the airport.

She stayed in the room that they provided her. The way her uncle's house was built was so strange. The house was split perfectly down the middle. One side of the house is shaped, made to look, and paid to look like a mansion belonging to a millionaire. The other half of the house is like a cottage, comfortable, down-to-earth, and much more homey; but some may say... 'quaint'. The rooms they offered her and her family were on the second side. She felt uncomfortable to think about stepping to the other side. Something about it felt wrong. It felt... fake and manipulative. She couldn't describe the feeling; only she looked past the one doorway dividing the two sides like she was looking into the open jaws of a dragon, flame burning under her skin making her blood boil with the urge to run to safety. She spent her time in the room. Listening to music with headphones. Alone. In silence.

Giggles stammering up the stairs. What sounded like a struggle, she could recognize that laugh, that talk, and that clumsiness from a mile away. Her sister had arrived. She wasn't alone, she was with her friend. A friend she had never met. They were given two rooms, so her sister and her friend slept together and she shared a room with her dad. It wasn't weird because she had slept with her dad when she was little and they still slept on springy squeaky mattresses on the ground every night. She also slept with her dad at her grandma's house every Christmas because every family shared a room. She didn't fuss, because she knew there was no other choice and she was polite. She was indeed just the guest.

The only time she left the room was for dinner. It was a classically simple dinner made for every guest in the house. With Vietnamese cuisine on the table, it felt like home. It felt welcoming. But she was very tired and could not figure out why. There was something that she felt a cautious, lingering feeling of. She couldn't put her finger on it. *It's definitely in her mind. There's nothing wrong. Move on, paranoid.*

Dragging her feet, she retreated back into her room and her dad stayed downstairs with her uncle. Her sister and her friend skipped to their room and were screaming and laughing at the darndest things. As girls do. She was listening to music. Alone. In silence.

She wasn't aware of when she fell asleep but she did. She was tired.

Do you know that lingering moment between being fully awake and being asleep? The moment where your senses are fuzzed yet active, where you are aware but slow to process. It is a sensation we all feel when we turn to press the snooze button, entirely aware of the fact we will oversleep but not being able to fully process that fact. We sleep on, or we wake up our processing systems slowly.

She felt his heat. Inching closer. Warmer and warmer, yet so chilling. Slithering around her, his arms tightened around her like bondage. Holding her tightly in his arms. Supposedly comforting, she couldn't figure out why she felt so much at unease. She sensed it all, but she couldn't process a reaction. Tightening, the python began to squeeze the breath out of her; every nerve in her body wanted to squirm, scream, something. But, nothing. Nothing happened. Her eyes couldn't even open, but she didn't need to. Her mind's eye recalled and recorded the whole thing from the interpretation of her other senses. His body up against hers, pulling her in for a side hug that was meant to render her useless. The warmth was overwhelming, heating up and burning her skin in an urge to run. She couldn't squirm, but he began to. His tailbone began to shift back and forth, clamping her leg between his clinging tentacles. *This is wrong. Move, Damnit. Get out of there.*

Huffing. His breath began to become uneven like an animal. He was hurling his body over her legs and grasping her upper body like a wolf heaving over its prey. Something about it so sensually sexual for him, but terrifying for her. She could sense her demise. She groaned. That was all she could manage to get out of her, and she turned. She turned to the side and tried to scoot a little ways away from him. Her body didn't give much. She couldn't do much, her body was still heavily paralyzed in her sleep paralysis and her shock. He let her go for a bit, only to inch closer once again.

She felt his heat. Inching closer. Warmer and warmer, yet so chilling. Like the snake and slithering creature he is, he wrapped his arms around her once again, but this time it was different. He reached his hands up her shirt. Feeling her. Touching her. Violating her. He grabbed and groped. He squeezed and seized. He treated her body like an object, he treated her like one. He grabbed her breasts, and she was rendered useless. The shock, the trauma, the fear, and the paralysis stopped her from having any hope. She had lost. She had lost everything including herself.

Her senses felt his breath unevenly blow the hairs on the back of her head. The tingle rolled down her spine, and her breasts felt pain. Everything felt pain. A numbing pain. Physical and mental pain to an unbelievable feat. *Daddy? Why?* Her voice muted.

The warmth shifted, now it was just cold. He got up and pulled the covers off of her. Cold. She felt cold and frozen-scared. He stripped her clothes off of her and she heard him neatly fold it to the side, like he had all the time in the world. Ears still listening, he pulled his clothes off. *No. Daddy, please.*

He pulled her close. He grabbed her legs and strangled his waist with them. Pulling her in. Touch is a cruel sensation. She could feel it. She could feel a hard, unforgiving python about to enter her system. But first. His turn. He placed his fingers in his mouth and then touched her. Felt her. Violated her. With some time, he moved his hands to tend to his python. Placing it up against her. Up against her flower. A delicate thing. Something that never did anything wrong. It didn't deserve that. The python never entered the flower, just placed pressure on it. The flower stood its ground. It wasn't destroyed, but it stood its ground. It was simply damaged after. It would never be the same. She was never the same.

He grabbed her breasts one more time and even placed his mouth on them. A horrid thing to do. And then he placed her clothes back on. Placed the covers back over her. And got up. And left. She cried.

She woke up and couldn't determine if she had imagined it all. Maybe it was her. She probably dreamt it, she was sick. Not him. She was viewing her father in such a negative and sexual light. How could she? What is wrong with her. She should never question if he would do such a thing, he wouldn't. End of story. It was her... then why did she feel so gross and violated. Why did she feel damaged from a dream?

She walked towards the bathroom and looked in the mirror. *It wasn't him. It was you. It was a dream. It is okay, just a dream. A dream can't hurt you. You weren't violated, it's in your head. You're sick.*

She dragged her feet towards her suitcase and got dressed for the day. She put on a pair of shorts and a tank top. She walked over to the mirror again. She felt so disgusted and gross. She walked back to the suitcase and changed. Blue jeans, a tank top, and a thick jacket in the middle of the summer in California.

She spent the whole day being dragged around by her sister, her sister's friend, and her dad. She didn't burden them with any of it but she consistently thought the whole day about the night before. Or was it that morning? She didn't know. The details were too hard to swallow. How could she dream such a thing? It had to be a dream right? If it wasn't, her sister and her sister's friend would have known. If it wasn't, her dad wouldn't be acting so normal. Right? It was just her. All in her head. Every nerve in her body wanted to call her mother to try to figure out a way to sort this out. But she didn't. *What if she thinks I am crazy? What if she gets mad at me for having these thoughts? But what if it actually happened, what would happen then? She would kill him.* But if she told her, everything would get worse. Her family was already having so many issues. She already was hiding so much from her dad. She couldn't tell him that her mother didn't love him anymore. She couldn't tell him that her mother was ready to leave him. She couldn't tell him and break his heart. But if she told her mother, her mother would leave him and kill him. *If it did happen, was it justifiable?* He hasn't been able to satisfy his sexual urges because her mom won't even let him touch her or be near her without fussing. *Was it justifiable? Was that why? No. wait. It wasn't real. It was a dream.*

A day of shopping. A run on the beach. A nice dinner. And back to bed. Her sister and her friend skipped to their room and were screaming and laughing at the darndest things. As girls do. She was listening to music. Alone. In silence. In the guest room. Drowning out the noise of the world and the noise in her head.

She wasn't aware of when she fell asleep but she did. She was tired.

It happened again. But this time a little different. This time, she knew it was real. It happened the exact same way, but the end... The end was different. His slithering fingers wrapped around her delicate hands. And he made her choke out the python. Choke the python until it spit. Until it splurged. Until he was satisfied. He used his hands and his clothes to try to wipe all of the python's spit off of her hands, and got up. And left. She cried. She woke up and ran to the shower. She locked the door to the room and also locked the bathroom door. She showered. She scrubbed. She scratched. And she washed her body all over with three layers of soap, tears, and time.

Knocking. Her sister was screaming through the door at her. She was mad. She was mad that she was taking too long in the shower and she couldn't go out to hang out with her friend without her. She was mad. And the girl? Well, she couldn't get clean. Even in the morning shower, she couldn't. It didn't scrub out. She was damaged.

She walked over to the desk.

She picked up the article and she began to read.

Chapter 21

MARKED

Sometimes she feels like her life had always been black or white. Like her whole existence, she'd seen the world in a black or white perspective; like a pair of sunglasses landed directly in front of her eyes, blocking the sunlight and brightness to shine into her mind. She couldn't see the color like Dorothy, she couldn't see the greatness that life had to offer.

With one swift move, her life was marked. A red hand print showed up on her skin; not hers. A red marking of someone else on her chest. At first it was a fingerprint. A small signing off on a package, a claiming of possession; not belonging to her. Then another showed up on her breast. Feeling a feeling she didn't want. Another marking her in an area even the sunglasses didn't allow the sun to go to. Handprints showing up all over her skin, all over her sins.

She can't help but feel like she deserved this. She had wanted to see color. She wanted to see the truth of the world; but she never asked for it, not from you. Did you violate her, or did she have something to do with how it happened? Did she do it? Was it her fault?

Eyes opening finally, you were gone. She saw every mark on her body, every shadow of where you touched her. She felt the white rain flowing through her fingers as she looked up at the sky to see if there were any clouds covering the sun. She only saw the void; no sky, no clouds, and no sun. She got up and went to the shower, trying to scrub every last mark off.

She can't see the red marks anymore; in fact she didn't see black and white at all anymore. She sees color, she sees the world for all the greatness it is and she appreciates everything; but at what cost? Because no matter how hard she tries, the world has color, but she has lost hers. The shadows, imprints, and scars of your touch will always be there. She sees them everyday. She sees them in herself, not even on herself anymore. Something new had been added to her identity, something she didn't choose but now felt mute;

#metoo

Chapter 22

BABY BIRD

We weren't close per se. In fact, I actually felt quite bad for her. What was her name again? Jean? Ya, Jean Louise (not her real name, but for the sake of this, it is). An odd name of sorts really, but one that you can never forget. Last year, freshman year, was her first year at Congressional School. Supposedly supposed to be the easiest year to transfer to a new school, the stage where everyone is starting over again and in the inset of highschool.

"Oh! Hey, my name is Wynn! Looks like we will be in the same advisory!"

It was orientation day. The new students had an entirely different orientation event in comparison to the rest of the freshman class, but I was chosen to help out at the event for the new students to 'form bonds' and 'create everlasting friendships' with these newbies that I had no intention of talking to ever again. I originally went into high school with one mission: get as much done to the best of my ability and be my own person ready to move on with my life. Nothing had changed. So, I had no intent on making 'lasting' friendships per se with anyone new; I simply had no time. I was taking a fully booked course load and admitted myself into several-upon-several clubs, with responsibilities of their own. But, I'll play nice I guess.

She just looked at me nervously. Took a quick glance at her name card, indicating that my statement stood true, and then feared to look at me and looked back down immediately afterward.

Interesting character... I didn't know how I felt about this girl, but she intrigued me. From what I could tell so far she was one with quite a lot of fear, caution, and she clearly wasn't going to have an easy time getting into the swing of the 'Congressional School way'. Whatever that way is.

"So, Jean? Is that right? That is an interesting name! Nice to meet you," I held my hand out to shake hers in mine. I did not receive a hand.

For the rest of the event, I paid close attention to this girl. Something about her made me want to continue to observe and analyze her. Something felt hidden, hurt, and like a poor baby bird that fell out of the nest into a new scary environment of snakes. I noticed this Jean girl had one acquaintance, who didn't seem to care for her. An acquaintance, I later approached to obtain more data in a sly manner. Turns out, they went to the same school, and were "friends". She did the air-quotes, I didn't. *I don't like you.* I'd talk more about her, but she's beside the point and doesn't matter much.

Soon the group merged in with the other freshman that had attended Congressional School for ages prior. The merging of lanes flowed easily for many, but Jean. *Oh, Jean.* Quiet to say the least. To say a little more: terrified of losing the one link she had, ultimately lost that acquaintance, and then in search of new help.

"So you use your... um... rowing sticks?" My attention is drawn to another conversation held between one of my oldest friends I drifted quite a ways away from and one of my closest male friends, who did rowing as a sport.

Stop moving for dramatic effect. Turn around to look at them with a questioning "wHaT dID SHe sAY" face. Cue line, "Did you just say... 'rowing sticks'? Do you mean 'oars'??" Nailed it. Laughter burst out of my two friends, and surprisingly enough, out of Jean too. From that point, I started to notice a closer attachment forming between me and Jean, but nothing extremely noticeable though. Just a new help kind of bond, until the next best thing shows up. Like a substitute.

We walked to our advisory and turns out Erial was in my advisory. Like a sudden readjustment of judgement, Jean quickly shifted her allegiance to the top energy of the room: Erial.

Here is the thing about Erial. Our relationship had a falling out of sorts. I'm trying to put it lightly, but my emotions are crystal clear about her and cut like a shard from a broken glass, granting me 5 years of bad luck so far. I consider myself quite lenient with people, I try my best to give people the benefit of the doubt. Any time between 5th grade to freshman year, Erial would manipulate me to feel obligated to do things for her because 'I was her friend', I would be benevolent and let it go. Any time she judged me or criticized me on my abilities in her 'areas of expertise', I thought, *she is just trying to do what is best for me.* Any time she thought I was a lot more book-smart in comparison to her; she'd complain about how she wasn't smart enough, praise me, and convince me to help her. She left me to become closer friends with other people and left me abandoned with no one, but whenever she needed someone to do something for her she didn't think she could manipulate out of someone else she would turn to me. I'd do it, no doubt. Despite knowing I got nothing out of the relationship, I did it. I still would. That is just because I highly believe in the concept that "what others do to you should not change who you are, you just go above it all and do better". I came to the realization of this toxic cycle and I figured that if she could find a new best friend and still lie to me that I was a close friend to her when she needed help, then I can find someone else too. And I distanced myself from her and her toxic, narcissistic, egotistical ass. Sorry, *strong* emotions. The joke is that she actually still believes that we are friends and I will still stoop down to her when she needs it. *HA!*

Sadly, like my mistake in 5th grade when I was Erial's first friend, Jean became 'best friends' with her. When Jean made that decision, I couldn't save her. I interacted with her, the same level I interacted with Erial: apathetically. I went on with my life and continued upon my mission, while, out of pure curiosity, once in a while checking up on my baby bird.

Chapter 23

LOVE?

I sat across from him.

I can't handle him sitting next to me. A nervous chill spreads from the tips of each of my hairs to my toes like a sickness on a mission. I try to lounge and relax in my chair. I can't let him know, I can't let him see how he makes me feel. As much as I try, my body starts to curl, condense, and close off.

Suddenly my ring seems more entertaining than him. I start to play with my ring on my finger. Spinning it, turning it, taking it off and on; I will lock my attention on this ring. I want him to understand and help me, but I can't stop thinking about my ring. I can't let him understand. I can't let him in. I just can't.

Control, breathe and grasp a sense of yourself.

He stares intently at me and with every bat of his eyelids I feel mine start to try to push my eyes back into my head. If I can't see, he can't see me; because that has always worked. No one has ever wanted to sit down and stare at me like that. No one has ever made me feel so uncomfortable by being nice and wanting to break down my walls. No one has ever cared so much I could cry because I wanted to run.

Control, breathe and grasp the confidence.

He licks his overly dry lips as an excuse to let out his uneasy breathing from its prison; only to swallow it back down immediately afterwards. He clenches his jaw unable to let out any words, and unable to relent his gaze.

He's nervous too. I see that now, but why? He has nothing to lose, I have everything to lose. What if he hates me after knowing me? Am I worth a thought in his mind? Do I deserve this feeling? Especially from him?

I look at him directly without losing eye contact to not lose this war of who will be vulnerable first. I've never lost, but something about him makes me want to. But I can't. I've tried so hard to have a winning streak, I can't just stop winning. I can't just get rid of my walls and control just because it's him. I can't.

Control, breathe and grasp.

He holds out his hand slowly on the table. He continues to look intently at me and he gives a nervous smile. I can't smile. I can't say a word. I slowly put my hand in his. Then I realize, the nervous chill of sickness ails him too. A smile breaks through on my face while a tear escapes the cage. My lashes and eyelids relent. He looks at me and lets out a relieving sigh. "Wynn… I have to tell you something… I love you and I will never stop caring about you".

Control, breathe.

Those words. Those words that mean so much more than he knows. "You can never stop me from caring about you and you can never stop me from worrying when you cry".

Control.

I looked at him pleading with my eyes for him to stop. "Because, Thành Phi, you are good enough and you are worth it". No. No. I can't hear those words. I have never thought of myself as being good enough or of any importance. I can't blame other people for not caring about me because I'm not worth caring about.

But he knows.

I don't need to tell him.

He knows my insecurities and he knows me. I push away. I let go of his hand and try to pull away. He grabs me back, and stares at my flooding eyes. "You mean the world to me and to everyone who knows you. You are enough and you have done so much. You are who everyone wants to be, and controlling your emotions is not why they look up to you. They look up to you because you are amazing, and you don't need to control, breathe, or grasp onto your life anymore. Because you can't control everything to help other people. For me, at least, breathe and be you."

I love him and he knows it. He is my friend, and I'm his friend. We have a love that is different from a simple romance, it is a platonic love where there are no limits. Where insecurities don't validate pushing each other away.

I can hear the whispers now. We learn from our experiences, and my experiences were screaming at me. Screaming the whispers of all my friends and all the peeping birds, "Oooooh, are y'all dating? He totally likes you. You totally like him. You should date! Oh mY gOd, you'd be so cute together!"

Thinking back on it, that would have bothered me years ago...

*   *   *

Something has to be wrong with me. I could feel the sweat formulating in my pores ready to be released. Wait, no. That's my tears.

"Well? Wynn, it was a simple question," the kids festered in their
seats like it was the question of the century.
"No one," I formulated a half-assed response in avoidance of
diving in any deeper.
"Stop lying. Who do you like, Wynn? Who do you like?"
"I'm not. Really. No one," I could feel my heart begin to crack and
show through my vocal quiver.

They don't mean any harm, I know. It has always just been a question I hated to hear during these games of truth or dare. In middle school, when we weren't playing tag games or recess games, we sat down and played games of truth or dare. I hated to do truths and formulated a bit of a reputation for myself as a dare devil. Secretly, it was to compensate for my chronic fear of stumbling across that trickwire of a question. Like little kid fun, that idea of crushes and butterflies seemed to be all that was important in our truths. Every time someone asked me that question, I could just feel myself want to run away. I knew I couldn't tell them the truth. They wouldn't understand or believe me, because I know I wouldn't either. They would think something was wrong with me, because I know I did. What was I supposed to tell them? The truth?

I had a million moments where I would imagine what would have happened if I had only been honest and truly trusted those around me at the time.

> *I have never had a crush. I have never had the feeling of wanting someone to kiss me. To comfort me. To love me. Or to even keep me company on the lonliest of moments. I have never felt an attraction towards another person so much that it made my stomach turn. I have never felt so much feeling of awe and adoration for someone to the point I can't stop thinking about them romantically. I don't know what it feels like to have a crush. I don't know what it feels like to stumble in front of another person because I just can't figure out what to say to them due to a cat catching my tongue. I don't understand the feelings, I don't know the feelings, and I don't know why. I know already. Something is wrong with me.*

Thank goodness I never actually responded with that. It haunted me and followed me around though. If you are a girl, you probably understand this, but a core bonding component to girl friendship is talking about boys and crushes. For me, it was more like an advice radio show. More advice giving, less sharing. At times, I would be put on the spot and I would spit out a lie and kick sand over it.

"What about you, Wynn? Like anyone right now?"

"Uh… sure," *Lie.*

"Oh My God, Whooooo?"

I would give them a cop out answer of my best male friend. Because I didn't understand the difference between the love I felt and the love they felt. I actually was once convinced that I had a crush on someone, because I wasn't careful with realizing there was a difference.

In 5th grade, Nosyla ended up attending Congressional School. It was super nostalgic to see her again; however, I didn't realize that I had become a different person already and that we no longer fit well together anymore. We still hung out a bit, but in 6th grade, I had become someone who liked to compete with this one male friend. Our friendship fostered a concept of competition and challenging. I enjoyed it and I felt myself creating a platonic bond that I assume was only special to me but not him.

Nosyla asked me one day, "Hey, I have a question. Do you like him?" The real question. I couldn't avoid it. "I don't know," I answered honestly. I didn't know what it felt like, and I assumed that since she had had crushes before she probably knew what she was talking about. I trusted her in the wrong area to make the judgement for me. And she told me, "I think you do. That's cute. You would be cute together, I mean you already are cute together now". Harmless words that made me contemplate everything. Maybe I should listen to her, maybe she knows my emotions better than me. *Boy, was I wrong.*

The thing is that without that feeling of actual romantic affection I felt no jitters, no nerves, and no hesitation. I sort of approached it similar to a task to complete, a box to check, a thing that could magically make me normal and complete finally. Without a moment to breathe, I just directly told this kid that I liked him and then, like little kid drama, that went around. It became a story to remember and that would be imprinted on my reputation until the next thing. I didn't feel hurt when he told me he didn't like me back. I didn't feel shame in confessing emotions, but instead I felt embarrassed for thinking that I did. I didn't. I was susceptible and vulnerable at the time because I constantly told myself something was wrong with me in that area, that I believed the first thing I was told could give me a chance to be normal. But it honestly just made me feel worse. It made me feel more shame for not being normal, because it just emphasized it more in my mind.

Fast-forward several years, I continued to contemplate my abnormality and actually wondered if it was a mental disorder. However, as I got older I became more exposed to the fact that there are more sexual orientations other than heterosexual. My friend came out as bisexual, and another came out as gay. I thought it was natural and normal. And love started to bloom everywhere; it got me thinking: *Could I be normal too? Could this be something with my sexual orientation?*

My freshman year of highschool, I found myself digging deep into the archives of the internet to see if maybe, just maybe, I wasn't abnormal. Research upon research upon research, I discovered that there was a sexual orientation identifying as Aromantic.

That year, I came out for the first time as Aromantic to two of my longest-lasting friends. Terrified, but I felt I needed to let myself breathe. I had felt like I was weird, unusual, and even like something was wrong with me for my whole life beforehand. "I have a crush," my friends would freak out about. I didn't understand. I don't know what butterflies you get when you meet a person. I don't understand the feeling of when you first see a person, you instantaneously imagine yourself in a relationship with them. Are we compatible? Are we perfect? And the etc. unrealistic ideals or fantasizing romance. I didn't get it. I thought something was wrong with me and I felt a bit left out at times, but I knew to feel comfortable with myself. I knew I was confident in who I was and I was proud of my pride.

So, when's the parade?

Chapter 24

BROOM IN THE CLOSET

I t's my sophomore year at this point. By the end of freshman year, I had a change of mindset. A year ago in December, my mom came out to my family about her cancer. With the emotions of everyone, everyone lashing out, I felt responsible to make sure everyone was okay. Middle-man of the day and to rescue the day. Then this past December, my mom *came* out. Like out of the closet.

My mom was driving me and my sister somewhere. The sound of her voice echoes in my head to this day, "You know if being a lesbian was legal when I was younger, you guys would not have been born."

That was a little weird of her to say.

"I don't love your dad anymore."

It was my responsibility to make sure she felt welcomed to the LGBT community and accepted as a human. I had recently come out to my mom and my sister as sexually identifying as Aromantic. Of course, it was only till recently that I found out that I am Greyromantic, not just Aromantic. Greyromantic is on the scale of Aromantic, but that's besides the point... Anyways, my mom and sister have been very big LGBTQIA+ supporters ever since then, but I truly didn't expect that kind of a turn. I helped her find out something that can free her and is a large part of her identity. I felt responsible; a responsibility no one bestowed upon me, I just took hold of the staff and crowned myself.

My sister and I found out about a female friend my mom made at the hospital. I don't remember exactly, but I recall my sister one day hushedly telling me she felt my mom was hiding something from us. Knowing my mom, I knew that confrontation makes her feel embarrassed and she wouldn't want to answer; so I let her tell me on her own time. Again, in the car, my mom told my sister and me that she had met this woman, much younger, at the hospital during her treatments for her cancer. This woman was a helper and also someone who seemed very sweet. My sister's response was quite negative and absolutely distraught; while I maintained a strangely calm, and completely emotionally shut off take on the situation. I found myself responding in a way I would for a friend, and promoted my mom for being a human. She is a human and deserves to be able to be attracted to whomever she likes; while deserving my utmost confidentiality with her business as I would do for anyone else.

I was *overwhelmed*. I was "coping" with a problem that really didn't exist. I shouldn't have felt responsible for anything, because nothing was wrong.

"Coping". What the *Fucking Hell* does that mean? Coping implies there is something I'm dealing with, something I can't fix so I have to learn to live with it, something that is still lingering on my mind, something that can't be dealt with directly. I'm not dealing with anything, Okay. There is nothing bothering me right now. I don't need you to *Fucking* give a *Shit* about me.

I'm Okay, *okay*?!

Why do you have to *Fucking* poke and prod into my business? You know what I think this is? You're just a *Bitch* who can't deal with their own problems and can't cope so you're telling me I'm the same as you. Well, I'm not. I'm not dealing with anything.

I just constantly think about killing myself. That doesn't mean I'm coping incorrectly. I'm not trying to compensate for anything. It's not like I feel like a nothing every day. It's not like when I was younger, my parents and family always called me stupid, and everything was my fault. It's not like I genuinely believe that I am not good enough. It's not like I try to push myself to constantly be better in everything because I want to finally hear they are proud of me. It's not like I blame myself for the fact that my family doesn't have another kid. It's not like my mom asked me if I wanted another sibling and I said no, making my sister and dad mad. It's not like I tried to become the son my dad always wanted. It's not like I used to identify as transgender when I was younger because of that. It's not like I still blame myself for turning out that way. It's not like I never felt like I was good enough and for some odd reason becoming a boy made me feel better. It's not like I began to guilt myself to think that I shouldn't be compensating for my mistakes that way but instead should have never made the mistake in the first place. It's not like I don't remember all of my childhood memories because of childhood trauma. It's not like my mom hid having cancer from my family for 2 years. It's not like my mom suddenly revealed it to my family a year ago. It's not like the year after, my mom came out to solely me and my sister that she was not straight. It's not like she has a 'friend' who is married with a baby. It's not like my dad didn't know for a full *Ass* year. It's not like it pulled on my heart when my parents stopped telling my sister stuff and solely me. It's not like everyone in my family basically asked me to lie to each other, while they just used me like family counseling. It's not like now I only see my mom once a week. It's not like my dad whines about no one loving him including me. It's not like my dad called me his best friend. It's not like I developed a small eating disorder. It's not like I am suicidal. It's not like I hate me.

So, *no*. I'm not thinking about something I can't deal with. I just feel numb, and want to die. That doesn't mean there is something I need to cope with.

Just hand me the broom. Grasping it intently, I'll sweep it up. I'm in control, with nothing to avoid or cope with; so just get out of the way and let me clean up this mess that collided out of the closet.

Chapter 25

BUILT BROKEN

Broken home in a built house
Fall out feelings in a fool-free farm
Realizing Salt in a freshwater state
Seeing the truth spilled out on a plate

Spoon fed belief in the truly discreet
Cursing culture in cursing light
Fight or flight fixed for life
Knowing right, knowing left
Knowing all will forget

Sewing seeds in the sheen
Worrying fetus in an ignorant womb
Child is smarter than the fumes

Bluffing fluff in the face of trust
Losing tradition in the listening
Formulating new in a sitting
Signing petitions
Writing lessons

Wynn Thành Phi

Listen
Watch
And
Buckle In.

Chapter 26

MAKE A WISH, JEAN-Y

"You get to go to I.S.A.S. this year," the coordinator for the band I was in informed me. I love this man, but now I love him so much more! He has always had a sense of humor similar to mine, and it was just a year ago when he approached me to recruit me without a need to audition. The aforementioned news might just be what I've needed. I need to get out of here, and I need something to finally feel excited about! I need an escape to avoid my reality and responsibilities at home.

I.S.A.S. Arts Festival: Independent Schools Association of the Southwest Arts Festival.

I had been a member of Essential Standards, the band at my school, for two years now and I was finally chosen to attend! I sing. Shocker! The most basic of all the instruments, my very own vocal cords. The very ones that saved my life more than once with a tongue quicker than a switchblade. Turns out it can sound like a blooming rose also, despite the thorns. I was on one song, but I was so overwhelmed with excitement for some change.

The one downside: Erial. Erial is in Essential Standards also, and unfortunately, she is praised as an innocent, puppy-like angel with a voice of a professional demonic rocker. Confusing right? *Who knows.* Everyone loves her, and it just feeds into her ego. She takes every moment she can to put the other members down, but like I used to, they take it as "constructive criticism". We literally started out the same in choir the same year, no offense, I know my voice better than you. **headshake** Whatever. She can't ruin this for me, even if she wanted to. I'll play nice though because at this point, I know I'll probably need to be in pairs to go around and she is the one I think would be easiest to cop-out.

"Hey, Erial! Wanna room together? We totally should! It would be so fun!!" *God, FAKE.*

"Oh My God, yes!! Me, you, and Jean should totally room together!"

I completely forgot that we needed four people to make a room. Ok, I guess that is fine. It is about time I check in on my little baby bird again, and who knows what could happen.

"OH MY GOD, YESSS!!" *sometimes you have to be over-enthusiastic with fake people.*

We planned on rooming all together with a fourth member. We ended up getting in the same room and we all packed and got to school ready to depart. I was ready to go.

Getting on the bus, I sat with Erial's brother, a sweet soul, and the first thing Erial said was, "Can I have the window seat?" *Puppy dog eyes.* Jean smiled naively and agreed with a nod. I sat in the aisle seat across from Jean. *Damn, she's tall.* Looking up to her, though we were sitting at the same level, I felt uncomfortable talking to her and Erial across the aisle. So, I turned to the alternative. *Texting.* Cue the annoying older person saying, "you kids. Always on your phones. Tsk tsk tsk". *I HAD NO OTHER CHOICE.* Also, it was an environment I could control easier.

I created a group chat amongst Jean, Erial, and me, prompting them to play a game I had made up ages ago. I call it: the Question Game.

Here are the rules of the Question Game:

1. Nothing leaves the conversation/chat
2. Leave room for indulgence in other conversations to better bond

3. And answer honestly, like it is a truth or truth game
4. Ask questions to each other, taking turns, and the questions can vary from whatever you want.

Quite a fun game in my opinion, because it suits everyone who plays the game. You can ask questions like ice breakers, questions about ranking people we know by how much we like them, or otherwise. I usually asked questions about more in-depth things to prompt answers that I could analyze to learn more about a person. The way someone answers questions without second thought says a lot about their personality. So the game was set and ready to play.

"I'll go first," Erial claimed. Jean and I waited for her question.
"Wynn, what is something you are most looking forward to at ISAS?"
Boring and predictable. "Well, I think probably being able to roam around and meet new people," I responded.
Ok, it was my turn. I'm kind of glad that Erial decided to ask me first, that way I could ask Jean. What to ask her though...
"Jean, just curious, what does your name mean and what is the origin of your name?" I've always had a fascination with names and names often tell a story.

The conversation began to pick up. Jean began to spill her little heart out on how her name wasn't always 'Jean'. She actually got it legally changed. Originally, her name was Susan, but everyone called her by her middle name, 'Jean'. She ended up getting it changed legally, and she started to talk about how, honestly, she really liked her name as Jean. She felt it suited her better and Susan was a name that she never really felt herself identifying with. It was quite a story, and from it, I saw her baby bird passionately singing about herself. She was someone who has been stripped of her ability to talk about herself a lot and seeing her be able to do so was pride in herself she had not portrayed earlier on.

"Oh, my middle name is Elizabeth! So I get that feeling of having an old grandma's middle name!" Erial opened her mouth. *Um. Why did you say that?*

"Haha ya," Jean quieted up again. Intriguing character, deserves more digging and data.

"If it means anything, I like your name. And I can't imagine you to be a Susan either, you suit your name, Jean. It is a nice name," I mentioned.

The game continued on throughout the whole bus ride and I gotta dig a bit more, but with every attempt towards opening Jean up to see who she really was, Erial made her take two steps back into her shadow. *Annoyed.*

We made it to the place we were going to stay for the trip, and we all went to our rooms to settle in and get ready for the first day! Honestly, I was a bit paranoid, because I had never really stayed with other people without my family before. To say the least, I was slightly wound up. Right off the bat, I stated, "I don't like to share a bed with anyone else. Hope y'all don't mind if I take the tiny couch?" No one minded.

The room was quite nice, lined with carpeting similar to a school: dark, tiled, rough on the skin, and questionable if it is entirely clean. Walking in, immediately to the right, the bathroom was brightly lit with two sinks and an awe-worthy mirror that spanned across to both sinks. Continuing onward, the bathroom and shower, conjoined, was hiding in the corner. The actual bedroom was further in, with two beds, equally spaced in the room allowing a pathway to walk. The beds were oriented the same against the wall that divided the room from the bathroom and was made cleanly in white linens that were crisply folded. On the opposite wall, the wall that faced the rest of the room and had the perfect view of the exit, the lonely small couch resided. It was a cute little thing that was made not as cushy as the beds or as boujee, but would do just fine. It was enough.

After getting all of our stuff settled in, we got dressed and went to the ISAS event.

On the first day, Jean was scheduled as one of the first things to perform. Jean was an actor and felt a thrill in theatre. Something, I honestly always commend, is people who can act; the memorization, the dedication, and the ability to manipulate yourself enough to adjust to the circumstance of the scene are honestly so amazing. It seems to take a lot of effort and there is a reason why it is an art, a skill even. Jean left to go to her set, and Erial and I were left in each other's company. Erial seemed preoccupied with the want to go and see her other friend from another school at ISAS. Her school hadn't even arrived yet.

"Um, I think we should go see Jean. We should go support her and also just enjoy it," I brought forth the concept to Erial to try to prompt her to think *she* wanted to go and think it was her idea.

Took some convincing, but finally Erial agreed to go and watch Jean. We walked side by side from our assigned school homeroom at ISAS towards the building where Jean's event was going to take place. It was still a little early; but "early is on time, on time is late, and late is unacceptable" as they say. There were two people standing guard in front of the facility, like royalty was inside and hopefully the show was solid gold. I had high hopes, and honestly, was looking forward to seeing my baby bird spread her wings like a Northern Royal Flycatcher bird. Erial, on the other hand, continued to seem preoccupied and didn't seem like she was anticipating much past the doors.

"Oh My God! I completely forgot something back in the homeroom! Hold my spot??"

Erial has the mind of a walnut, so nonexistent. She oftentimes seems quite forgetful and doesn't take into account how that forgetfulness takes a toll on other people's time and other people's feelings. The number of times Essential Standards has had to hold off on rehearsals because she forgot something is too many times to count. The productivity of the group gets held back, but no harm. No one judges her. *Not My Problem.*

"Sure," I watched as Erial begin her little sprint that quickly devolved into a fast walk. She headed up the path back to the room to get who knows what.

At this point, I was standing outside the facility, stared at by the two personnelles outside like a piece of dead meat and two vultures. I felt uneasy. Suddenly a small voice in my head decided to speak up, *sit down. You will be waiting a while.* So as instructed, I propped up against the wall and scooted my butt slowly down to the ground. The two vultures glared and judged.

After waiting for what felt like an eternity outside in the blaring sun, the vultures allowed me to pass the red, velvet rope, only to be blocked again at the closed doors. I inched up towards the doors and was eagerly awaiting them to open. At this point, I have waited so long for both this performance and for Erial to return, I sure hope this was worth it.

"Hello, are you here to watch the One Acts too?" an aggressively soft spoken voice reached out to me from behind.

I turned around to see a new face to me. A petite sized girl in light blue ripped jeans and a white flowery ruffled top was standing behind me. Her demeanor and approach was one of a lacrosse player and she had an essence that felt like someone who was outgoing and well-liked by many. Her hair was dark, but not black. Her face was quite angular and had an appeal to it that could mark it as attractive to the eye. Her voice, however, was one of demand, power, and aggression that hid under a delicate, light demeanor.

Conclusion: someone who is popular, sporty, and outgoing in a way that she can obtain what it is she aims to achieve; finally, she is someone new to obtain data to collect.

Oh. She's staring at me. I should probably respond. "Yes, I am. I am here to see the One Acts that is being performed by my peers from Congressional School."

"Wait, you go to Congressional School? I don't, but my sister does. That is why I am here to watch," her outgoing nature began to show.

Erial finally showed up just in time as the doors began to open right after her response. Walking in, the whole room was dark, and there were a whole set of folding theatre seats in the abyss within the facility. Walking in Erial looked to me and whispered, "Who is that? I kind of don't want to sit next to her." *Um.* I didn't want to think too much into it, and didn't want to sit down to explain to Erial how messed up what she just said was, so I just told her to go first. Being just us three in the audience, we sat together. Erial on my left and this new character on my right. We still had some time to spare, so I looked over to my left to try to spark up conversation with Erial, but she was on her phone looking at instagram. *Not interesting.* I turned to my right.

"Sorry, you said your sister is in the One Acts? Who is your sister?"

"Haha, ya, my sister is in the One Acts. I don't know if you know her though. She's a senior this year," this girl responded.
"Wait. Are you Lina's sister?!"

I knew Lina, a senior at the time, because she was in my sister's grade and, as well as, she was dating one of my other close male friends at the time. She was a shy little bug and I absolutely adored every time I talked to her; but, sadly, not everyone agreed with my assessment. All of her grade disliked her and bullied her, while the rest of the highschool students ignored her. She found comfort in the arms of my close friend, and shortly after they started dating. Though I was never extremely close to her before, I found myself wanting to get to know her and ending up really liking her quirky company. Most judged her, because she had a different understanding and preference in her love language. I am not one to judge, I actually love to see when she fully embraces her weird, fun-loving self.

"Ya! That's my older sister! How do you know her?" in surprise, this girl didn't think that I would know her sister.

From the side of my eye, I felt a slight movement and a loss of light. And suddenly I heard a voice bafflingly terrify me off-guard.

"Wait, you're Lina's sister? Like Lina, who is dating Dew Itty?" Erial's attention had been sparked.

"Yes," the girl kindly responded.

"Oh My God, Dew Itty is my friend! I can't believe you are her sister! I have a question though, because I'm kind of curious: are they as intimately close when they are around you or your family as they are usually?" Erial mouth uttered.

"Of course I know her!" I interrupted the conversation, because I wanted to not embarrass Lina with her sister; especially of things maybe she didn't want or she shouldn't know, "I absolutely adore her, and always have. My sister is in her grade as well, they aren't friends though. I am friends with your sister and also friends with her boyfriend. I think she is adorable and they are adorable together! I really love hanging out with your sister and being in her company. I think she's quite a catch of a friend and person... Wait, what is your name?" I prompted the girl to allow the conversation to move forward because our time waiting for the show was limited and coming to a close. Erial turned back into herself and I noticed the light source return in the corner of my blindspot. Back on her phone, I suppose.

"My name is Fiona. I am just a freshman. I'm glad you like my sister. From what I hear, not many people like her. We are complete opposites, ya know. I consider myself outgoing and people often like me a lot, but Lina is kind of the opposite. Ya, no one likes my sister, I get why. Often, people can't imagine us to be related."

"I get that! Obviously, my sister and I are only two years apart, but we are exact opposites too. My sister is more on the outgoing, well-liked by everyone, and likes to socialize a lot, while I like to be alone more often, am extremely introverted, and get along well with your sister. I understand for your sister, so I often like to stand up for her! But to be honest, I don't see how people can't see you two are related. You both actually are quite similar in the way your personalities are. You are both quite kind and unique. I hope you both get along well."

"We definitely do! I love her with my whole heart! Sometimes I wish she would act differently though so she isn't bullied or hated so much though."

"Honestly, I don't wish that for her. I think she is a strong independent individual who will do so much with her life because of the fact she isn't willing to change for anyone else."

"That's a fair point... I'm glad my sister has you on her side."

The lights began to dim down, and Fiona and I bid our farewells to our ending remarks and the show began.

*   *   *

Walking out of the facility, the show had just ended. We bid our goodbyes to Fiona, and I never saw her ever again. She vanished as quickly as she had arrived, like a ghost.

"What did you think of the One Acts?" I asked of Erial.

"They were good," a brief statement of response as she looked upon her phone, robotically scrolling, and walking misguidedly away.

Just GOOD?! How about amazing?! Phenomenal?! Engaging?! Or at least say something about Jean??!! I personally felt that, though I did mainly go to see Jean, everyone's performances were amazingly done! Jean was the best though. That may be because I am biased in what I wanted to see, a baby bird spreading her wings like a beautiful blue bird!

"Um, Erial? Where are you going?" I had already stopped trotting
along, but Erial continued to walk dysfunctionally away.
No response. Just blindly continuing to walk away.
"Erial, don't you think we should wait for Jean to finish cleaning
up and come out to join us? So she doesn't walk alone?
And doesn't feel like we abandoned her?" I suggested
shyly, because honestly I was conflicted within myself as
what to do.
"Oh My God! My friend is here! I gotta go see her!" Erial didn't
hear a word I said, did she. I sure hope it is that she
didn't hear me or was ignoring me, and not that she didn't
care about Jean. That can't be it, she definitely just didn't
hear me.

Time for me to choose. Morality wise, I can't leave Jean behind,
I'd rather her not walk out alone and not know where to go. On the
other hand, if I don't get a move on soon, Erial will have already
walked off a ways away and there is no way for me to catch up
with her. If I stay and wait, Erial, Jean, and I would all be alone for
a period of time and lose that buddy system. What should I do?
AHHHHHH! *Panic*

I decided to run along after Erial, because I definitely didn't want
to be alone for any bit of time and I didn't want Erial to be alone
either since we were together already. I did feel bad though. My baby
bird was going to leave the facility and wonder where we've gone. I
just wish I could send her a little brain wave message to let her know
what is going on. *Sorry.*

"Wait up!" I shouted after Erial.

We walked farther away down the path; however, now, Erial
wasn't the only one who was distracted. As her mind drifted to her
friend, mine drifted and allowed my heart to reside with Jean. I hope
she doesn't feel too hurt. Or I hope she doesn't feel lonely. Or I hope

she doesn't feel like her only friends, that she thought were there for her, could easily leave her behind just like that. I wasn't as close to her, but I don't want her to feel that way. I would never want her to think that she is so disposable to the people she thought cared. There is no way Erial would do that on purpose to her friend, right? She definitely has to care about Jean, at least more than she did for me. Jean deserves better. Erial has definitely grown since then, right?

"Oh My God! There she is!" Erial projected more excitement in seeing this friend she had no close connection with than she did with Jean, someone she came with.

Introductions took place, but I honestly didn't feel inclined to analyze this new character. I think they were talking, but I honestly don't know. We also were still walking, I think. My mind and heart weren't in it. *Guilt-ridden.*

Bvvvvvv! BVvVvvVV! BVVVVVVVVVVVVV!!! Must have been Erial's phone vibrating… or it could have just been my heart ringing and sinking in, my own inner guilt clock notifying me of my last few seconds before the guilt kills me. And then *KaBlam!*

She HUNG UP! SHE JUST HUNG UP! Erial ignored it, and I felt that it would be rude for me to confront her about it in front of her friend. My mind had too many things going on at the same time and my decisions felt immoral. Is there something I could be doing?

Bvvvvvv! BVvVvvVV! BVVVVVVVVVVVVV!!! Click. Hung up.
Bvvvvvv! BVvVvvVV! BVVVVVVVVVVVVV!!! Click.
Bvvvvvv! BVvVvvVV! BVVVVVVVVVVVVV!!! Click.

All I could hope is that Jean stops calling Erial and just calls me. *Call me. Please. Jean. Please.*

Ding! That was my phone this time. Wait, did it work? Did I actually just send her a little brain wave? Did she hear me? I looked down and pulled out my phone.

"Jean Louise"
She texted me.

"Hey Erial! Jean texted me! She asked where we are," I disregarded

Erial and her friend's conversation they were having. This
seemed more important. Erial would care, right?
A simple nod. Ok. Um. I don't know what to do with that.
"I'm going to text her where we are," I responded. *A simple nod.*
Erial and her friend continued to walk and talk.
"Wait! Hold up! I think we should stop moving, so Jean can find
us," I suggested a solution that seemed self-explanatory,
but I guess I had to say it.

They stopped moving and we waited for Jean. Suddenly this
random friend said, "Actually, I gotta go! We can see each other later,
but I do have to go now since I'm already late to prepare for my set!
Great to see you again and get to meet you, Thành Phi! Hope to see
you both again soon!"
Jean joined us once again soon after, and once again, Erial had
disconnected and her mind and attention drew back to her phone.

"Why didn't you answer my calls?" Jean chirped at Erial innocently
and hopeful of a sufficient answer.
"Oh My God, I must have not gotten them! I didn't see any calls!
Sorry!!" *Lie.*

Erial just... just... blatantly lied to Jean! I should probably say
something right about now, right? But Jean seems to feel okay with
that answer, so is it worth it to tell her otherwise? Ruin her view of
Erial? No. It isn't. I can stand firm on this decision. If Jean is going
to see it, she has to choose a better path for herself, I can't interfere...
or at least not like that.
The rest of the day went along quite boringly to be honest, and
there wasn't anything of great importance. To summarize it briefly, I
had no time to truly talk to Jean alone or in depth about herself, but
instead, we both just ended up tailing Erial around all day looking
for her friend, meeting up with her friend, and/or wondering where
her friend will meet Erial next. I didn't have complaints about not
getting to do other things other than look for this random girl who

apparently was friends with Erial, but I did feel annoyed at the fact that I had no time to indulge in my own meeting of new people. That was *annoying*. Or at least, can I explore my baby bird some more?

> "I'm hungry, we should go get some food," Erial seemed to always be hungry, but this time her stomach's timing was correct. It was lunch time, and lunch was being served in the far tent away from everything else.

At this point, Erial's friend had vanished once more, so it was just the three musketeers following the designated leader. Jean and I aimlessly followed, and we walked the long trail to the tent to pick up some lunch. The white gigantic tent resembled one of a circus tent, with a part of the roof draping over the sides, carving out slits as walking passages. Inching in between the crevices in the drapes, we saw the tables all aligned like a data table. All the way on the other end, there were tables lined up like a conveyor belt system in factories, however, we had to move along to pick up the food. A buffet of sorts. There were several different lines of tables with different foods, and you were allowed to move freely to grab and engulf whatever you seem to desire out of the options.

Maybe it is a cultural thing or I was brought up differently, but usually, with meals outside of my home, I eat minimalistically. I tend to choose the easiest options to eat, the cleanest options to consume, the fastest option, and the option that is the least amount of trouble. I always felt myself doing so instinctually, despite being told that I should just indulge. I just feel it to be polite and also, that way I don't have to stress about making a wrong impression with the way I eat. It is really something that has been embedded in the way I am. This applies here, at ISAS, at school, at family reunions, and anywhere outside of the privacy of my own home and safety.

I *have to* assume not everyone is brought up on that, because Erial and I went to two very different food lines and picked up very different meals. Jean, inevitably, felt obligated to choose one person to follow in a line with and chose Erial. No hard feelings, I was really just concentrating on getting my food and quickly going to sit down to scarf down the food and move on. Maybe I just don't like the idea of social eating,

I grabbed the corn doused in corn water, neighbored by some green beans. My plate wasn't nearly full, but I felt it'd suffice for the time being. Walking over to the station for drinks, I looked at the labels for the coolers and kept conscious of my blindspot where Erial was keeping up the line and Jean was walking slowly behind her grabbing much less than her. Now, new question: *Apple Juice, Milk, Orange Juice, Lemonade, or Water?* I think I'm going to go with bottled water. That way it is something I can carry around afterwards in case I get thirsty. Think smart, not hard. Erial and Jean found their way over and caught up with me and then we headed out to the grassy field in the sun instead of inside with the tables. I love sitting on the grass and the ground, something about it, might I say, is *grounding*. The healthy grass in the bright warm sun still is able to maintain their fresh appeal despite the soccer balls flying around and kids cartwheeling in enjoyment all over it. Sitting in a free area, Erial, Jean, and I begin to eat.

"Oh My God! There are bugs! It is really nice out here, but there are bugs. Should we sit inside instead?" Erial brought forth a challenged request.

"Actually, I really like it out here! Also, this way we have lots of open space and can even talk to the other students around us to just get to know them! I think we should stay out here," I responded quick-handedly, because I refused to move.

"Oh. Ok," Erial backed down because Jean did not make any remarks to take her side.

There were so many people around, but the energy of it all was exhilarating! The positive smiles, laughter, and pure happiness could simply be felt in the vicinity of the other kids hanging out and playing games. It was really honestly quite uplifting. A nice change of pace.

"So, what did y'all get to eat?" I decided to spark up some conversation.

Erial took control and responded first by showcasing her chicken, corn, mashed potatoes, green beans, and so much more. And then afterwards, Jean showed her small plate of a few strings of chicken and some green beans. Jean didn't seem to eat much, or she may just not feel as comfortable around Erial as she and/or Erial claim her to be.

"Wanna play a question game?" I continued onward. *Stuff mouth.*
Head nod of excitement from Jean. Maybe I'm reaching Jean and
    am not knowing it.
"Ha ha, ok. Then Jean, since you know how it works now, you go
    first!"
"um... Erial? How did you meet your friend??" Jean asked.

Erial went on a long tangent about her adventures. Her chances and opportunities to be able to leave the school environment, and paying to get her the chance to perform with other people, formulating new bonds and friendships! Seemed fun and interesting, but I was busy. All I noticed or learned from that conversation was a baby bird seeking an answer to *why*. *Why* did Erial shift her care so easily to someone else so easily? *Why* did Erial care more about this other person? *Why* did she feel so abandoned? And *why* does she feel so hurt about something she felt unworthy of feeling hurt about? A baby bird chirping silently through her body language and the quiver in her voice. Flapping around next to a snake, asking for help; but ultimately being ignored or eaten alive without the answers.

"That's interesting. Erial you're turn, ask someone a question," *moving on.*
"Ok! Ummmm... Oh ok, so Wynn, biggest pet peeve?"
Wow. Way of digging deep. I say that, but what *is* my biggest pet peeve? Many things annoy me, many things get on my nerves. People talking for me, people using other people I care about, manipulation, and so many other things. I feel like I get annoyed often, and at times

I have a short fuse that is well-hidden until I snap like a branch in the wind of the storm. But what would be useful to say right now? Which one will get the most out of this conversation?

> "I guesssssssss, it would definitely be when people I care about manipulate each other," *pause for effect, check your audience,*
> "I know that doesn't sound like a pet peeve, because it isn't like I'm getting annoyed at a constant click of a pen; but it is my biggest pet peeve. Because it is something out of my control, I'm not involved, and also it is lowkey annoying to the eye to see someone I love hurt someone else I love. Being aromantic, I feel platonic love more deeply..." *Baby bird looking at me endearingly, I think she's hooked.*
> "And I genuinely feel a certain level of hurt physically in my chest when I feel like my friends are destroying each other. Maybe it isn't physical and can't be seen, not even by the person being manipulated, but that doesn't mean I don't see it, and don't feel it, ya know?"

Immediately, Erial responded with a bland answer of understanding, "ya, I get it". A lie I wasn't even going to dive into. Erial is precisely why I started to formulate that pet peeve. I have taken on the maternal figure and the protective role because of her. Or was it because of her? Maybe I'm giving her too much credit. It was her, my parents, my sister, and everyone I have ever known. I can take it, I know I can. I have. But when I see someone else go through it, it annoys me and hurts. I can't watch someone else feel like they *have* to go through that. No one does. It isn't fair.

Looking over to Jean, her face quickly changed from an expression of awe and longing from what I said to one of neutrality again, right after Erial's comment. She truly seemed like she wanted the protection I was talking about. She wanted to reach out, but was unsure if she was good enough to qualify for the position. Like she wanted to fly out of the snake's nest, but wasn't sure if she'd be able to fly to the warm hand I was extending to her. *Don't worry, Jean. Friendship is never a one way thing, I'll slowly approach the nest closer and closer and the flight won't be as intimidating or lonely. Just wait for me.*

The rest of the meal went along swimmingly. To be entirely honest, I lost interest and my thoughts drifted to the positively calming energy of the environment. Sprawled on the ground. I layed down and looked at the bluest sky I had ever seen. Maybe, it was because I felt I could finally breathe, or it was because I never had a chance to breathe when I was at home. I was never given the opportunity. Something about that blue sky, made me wish that I could fly to be taken away by the clouds. Chatter happening next to me, Jean and Erial continued the question game. Sinking deeper into the ground, my body finally relaxed and real-life giving oxygen was breathed into me and let out a sigh through my mind. I closed my eyes.

Fast forward to day two, the start was boring. The action really started during lunch once more; then again I might be biased, because I knew that would be the only time I could reach out to Jean.

> "Hey! I hope you guys don't mind, but I won't be joining you guys for lunch! I'm going to eat with my friend!" Erial felt it wise to make last minute plans and leave at the last minute in order to eat with her friend. She left even without a response.

I don't mind really, because she has her own mind and has full control of her decisions, she can take her responsibility with her and do as she pleases. I have no control over that and don't care too much. Also, at this point, Erial had already been prioritizing her friend over Jean and I so many times, I really decided to not care about the buddy system anymore. She can do whatever she wants and walk alone to find her friend. Jean and I will do just fine.

I may have claimed that *too* soon… I looked over to Jean, about to ask her if we should just go ahead to lunch. Pure terror. Fully horrified and the color sucked right out of her.

"Um, Jean? Do you want to go ahead and go to lunch?" I hoped that my words could reach her, but based on the way it was looking, she looks parallyzed in shock and terror of doing anything without Erial. *Pause. Moment of silence.*

"I guess…" Jean finally responded.

I started to walk towards the lunch tent, taking note every few minutes of whether or not Jean was still following me. She was but she was similarly limping along slowly after me warily. I looked at her and made sure that she was listening to me when I told her that we should take her separate ways to go get lunch, and then meet outside afterwards. I didn't want her to feel like she had to follow me the whole time, and I wanted her to be able to have the freedom to grab whatever she wanted because she was her own individual person. And I don't like to feel responsible for her like I was in command of her.

We both went out enjoying each other on the grassy land and Jean looked like she had something that she wanted to get off her chest. I couldn't describe how I knew, I just knew. Maybe it was the look in her eyes, that look all too familiar to me, because I have seen that look in myself before. Or maybe she just had a cry for help that no one else heard, but I did. I reached my hand closer to the baby bird and she jumped willingly into the warmth that I provided.

"i just… i just…" Jean started but stopped.

"What's up? We can talk about it, there is nothing wrong with that. It's just you and me," I smiled kindly at Jean and let my metaphorical hand out to her.

"I just don't think it was fair of Erial to just leave us," Jean started to speak with the fullest volume of her voice. I don't think I've actually heard her speak fully before. The true song of the adult bird humming along a passion absolutely different from every other.

"Oh it definitely wasn't, but you know, Erial does that often. But ultimately it's okay though, we can have just as much fun!" I responded.

102

That proved to be right. We played a question game that took many fun tangents. Conversation of each other's hobbies, each other's interests, laughing at the foolish boys playing frisbee and doing so flailing, and even about the boy Jean so desperately liked. Her heart poured out in a way that I could only describe as "about time". It felt as if Erial had never stopped to actually listen to Jean or even stopped to see what Jean wanted.

An innocent conversation about boys didn't even seem to be on Erial's radar at all, even though clearly her friend, Jean, really enjoyed a nice, carefree conversation about how goofy a boy is. It had no standing value, but it was fun to talk about and laugh about the idiocy of the opposite gender. Although I don't relate in the romantic attraction to these beings, I did know how to analyze people and have many more interactions with them than Jean has had. This boy, in particular, was someone I actually was quite close with this boy was Nadim. So I could share many stories and interactions, and I could finally hear the genuine laughter of Jean. Strangely, Erial claimed herself to be closer with this male, but she didn't seem to share these experiences with Jean. *Weird.*

"Has Erial never talked to you about him?" I was laughing and
    questioning to test the waters.
"No, not really," Jean's face resulted in a resting smile.
"That's weird. She knows him better than I do, or at least I thought
    so. Because like they've been in a musical group together
    for years before I ever became friends with him. I find it
    surprising she hasn't talked to you about him at all."
"Who knows. I haven't had this kind of fun in a while to be
    honest," Jean revealed the honesty to me, and I knew I
    made a breakthrough to her. *Jean came to me.*

The conversation went onward, and it felt more genuine than anything that had happened prior the rest of the trip. A while later, nearly near the end of the lunch time block, Erial joined us once more. I feared that Jean would immediately go back to following and blindly stumbling after Erial again, but surprisingly, she didn't. Jean had an instant connection with me, and she started to gain a certain sense of confidence that I felt radiate in the colors of her feathers. My baby bird had learned to fly, and I was just blessed to see the progression. From then on, she stuck close to me and learned that her relationship with Erial was not a friendship she wanted or was good for her.

Chapter 27

LATE NIGHTS

I don't know what's going on with me.
I don't even know how I feel. The world feels like it's just moving on without me and I'm stuck in a loop going on and on and on. My own personal Ferris Wheel, my own personal death trap. And it's all *my* fault. Everything that's happened I deserve it. Or I think I do, I think I don't, I'm not even sure. I just don't feel anything anymore. I used to have at least a sense of knowing that I was feeling something, but now I feel nothing.

Nothing, it means whatever it is you want it to mean. It's an abstract feeling of absolute void, something you can never truly understand or describe. At the moment, I feel like I'm in my own personal void, my own version of *nothingness*. There's no way out and I don't even know how I got in. It's no one's fault. No one is to blame. There's no one to point a finger at, and that's the worst part.

The human mind automatically tries to find something, to blame something, to understand and reason why everything is happening; but some things just don't have something to blame. The human mind tries to wrap itself around the idea that some things happen outside of our control, but can still affect us without being anyone's fault. The mind soon turns on itself and you end up hating who you are. And that feeling soon turns into a sense of nothingness and numbness that you can never get rid of.

Everyone tells you that that feeling goes away; everyone tells you that it's just a phase and that you will move on, but it just doesn't feel true. Their words don't ring true, because at the moment you're still stuck in that *'phase'* and no one can save you from your own brain. You have to fight a war with yourself. And in the end, someone will lose and someone will win. For me, the war calls forth My brain versus My heart, and I'm afraid that either one winning won't be a good thing. My heart winning would mean that my heart would lose its sense of understanding, its sense of trust, and My sense of love. My brain winning would mean My sense to live is cut down to its one lingering thread. And in both cases, I don't want to lose anything or hurt anybody.

I don't want to lose.

No matter how many times people tell me that they're there for me, no matter how many times people tell me people are willing to fight for me; I don't want them to. I don't want them to feel what it is I'm feeling. I don't want them to understand what I'm going through, because what I'm going through I would never wish upon anyone else. I don't want to worry people, I don't want them to care; because when they care they become an excuse for why I live. And that's a lot of pressure.

I don't want to lose, but I don't want help.

I look at so many happy people around me. Their satisfaction in themselves marked by whether they have a significant other. You know high schoolers, the most important thing to them is social standing, and often having a significant other marked you for the top spots. Or maybe it was because they needed someone to lean on, that's why they look for those relationships. It's not like I need it. In fact, I don't even want it. I don't care for the social standing, I never have and never want to. But, the other thing... No, I don't need it. I don't even crave it. I don't even think that it's the fact that I desperately want it.

I don't need the satisfaction of having "a boyfriend" or "a

girlfriend"; I just want someone. Maybe it's my pride, my ego that gets in the way. Maybe it's my confidence, maybe it's something else; I just know that I don't look for it and I don't obsessively hunt it down like prey in a rat trap.

I don't obsess over the idea of needing to find a significant other. In fact, the thought never really crosses my mind naturally. It's just that sometimes I question if that want or automatic need that other people seem to suddenly have in their brains to formulate crushes, and etc.; if the fact that I am lacking that makes it unfair or illogical for me to ever want someone to just be there so I can feel I can just fall into their arms and be weak.

Take a break.

And not have to be the hero of my own story; even though I choose and want to be that very hero.

I guess I understand where that stereotype of not knowing what girls want in a relationship is so highly seen and stereotyped because in all reality no one really knows what they want. They just want someone who knows. *Just knows.* And I know that that can't happen, no one knows what you want and less you tell them; no one can read your mind. I don't need that. I don't want that. I don't search for another being to help me, I don't search for a significant other; if it happens it happens.

But sometimes I wish for that sense of trust I am lacking because I can't seem to understand what is running through the wheel in my brain. What Rumplestiltskin in my mind is spinning into what should become solid gold when understood. I don't understand but I will wait patiently for that hay to turn to gold, the day someone will catch me when I fall out of my rapunzel esk tower after years of being my own hero.

Until then, I have to hold my head high on my own. *Keep it together.*

When they come along, they'll hold my hand, hold me close. Give me a hug I won't refuse. Hold me in a way that I have always wanted so I can just melt. Someone who finally makes me feel a sense of relief to replace the constant tension my muscles keep intact. Someone. Anyone.

Yet no one.

Let's be accurate here: I'd never let that happen. I can never allow myself to see myself so vulnerable as to let someone else hold me. I can't ever see myself relent that feeling of being in control and being the one to get everything fixed. No matter if I want it, I can't have it. I won't let that happen.

Cry. Just do it. It's simple really, it's normal. Just cry already.

It would help. But the I turned to a she, and I looked upon myself and watched hopelessly. She struggled to try to muster up even a single tear, but she couldn't. Her eyes were dried up like prunes and her heart was shattered like broken glass her feet were bleeding from, as she trudged along.

"Hey it's okay to admit you want to cry"

As if she wasn't trying to; if only she could, then they would stop pestering her about her **feelings**. As if they really cared. She knew the truth, they were just waiting to see her cry and be vulnerable so that they could be the hero. All she wanted was to get that over with and continue to suppress her "oh *so* **important**" feelings.

"You know crying isn't healthy for you? Sometimes that is the best way for you to express your emotions, which are always a valid reason to cry,"

*God, I just wish I would shut up and leave it be. Just cry already. Just one tear and this nightmare of **care** will be over. Just stop caring!*

Was the fact that she couldn't cry saying something? Did the voices even truly care if she cried? The voices in her head pestering her to cry but did they really know what was best for her? For all she knew, they could be the ones keeping her from crying. If only she could just cry.

Why does she feel lonely?

She was fine literally a second ago. She felt that she was smiley, cheery, and solely pleased to be alone. She was comfortably and snuggly laying in her sheets watching Netflix on her computer. The brightness of her computer screen brightens her night; she felt happy adjacent where she felt like she at least was not feeling anything negative.

I'm not sure if she's feeling the way she feels because she needs to sleep now or something to that extent. She's just sleepy, tired, and exhausted. It is past 2 in the morning, after all, I think that need for sleep is all she's feeling.

It's all my fault.

She realized everything that is happening to her right this minute she somehow deserved. She had to have deserved it. She did everything wrong, she is to blame. Her parents are unhappy with the family because of me. Her sister is upset and she didn't do enough to help. She should have. Her dad was lost, she should have helped him. What happened shouldn't have happened if she just took responsibility.

I have no friends.

She felt she didn't have any friends. She pushed them away and they stayed away. She did this. She broke my heart. I broke myself.

And it's absurd that I feel that way. I shouldn't. I know it's not true.

But I believe it deep inside my core.

I *can't help it.*

Just another day in the life of depressive late night thoughts.

It doesn't get any easier.

Chapter 28

EASIER

It would be so much easier
If I just hated you.

Despising your demeanor
Hoping you'd never be here
Yelling, screaming, blaming you
For feeling
Like you hurt me
It would be easier to see
A world where you and me
Defeated
If only I just hated you.

Could you have been meaner?
So I could seem sure
Like knowing if you wronged me
I could feel the calm leave
I could throw a tantrum
Like you had a scandal
Knowing full well

you'd never let befell
Such a horrible thing upon myself
If only I just hated you.

It would be so much easier
Leaving you for the others to take
If only
I could just
Hate
You.

Chapter 29

THE PAIN IN LOVE

Honor thy father and thy mother.
To say the least, I have an interesting relationship with my family. I feel torn between love and pain; not knowing if the hurting is normal. My mom told me once that it is not easy to earn my love; but once I do love, I love more than what is good for me. The only people I give my love to, without them actually properly earning it, is my family; the only people that you'd assume would never do anything to hurt you.

In retrospect, why do we do that? Why do we blindly give our love, loyalty, and all to these people we are simply related to? Other than being related, where does that obligation come from? It could simply just be a social and evolutionary component that helps in our survival and our herd like instincts as mammals. Since the beginning of time, humans have been known to work as 'herds' and collaborate in ways to help ourselves and others survive in the wild. Varying from fighting off wildlife or other humans, the family unit's loyalty and unity gives them leverage to have a chance of survival. Think of it this way: do you have a better chance of surviving a shark alone or when you have more people? More people. Definitely, because it is a well known fact that to avoid getting attacked by a shark, you need to stay with a group. The family unit is the strongest form of a unit/ group. Or, *logically*, it should be.

No one talks about the emotional tolls, the inevitable falling out, and the negative things that come from family. Heard of daddy issues and mommy issues? How about the classic trust issues? Or childhood trauma? Ever heard of dissociation and disconnection? Ever heard of Dissociative Identity Disorder?

I couldn't do it anymore. I need to get out. Scrambling in my brain, I can't hear or focus on anything my parents are arguing about. I can't even hear or focus on my own thoughts, they are there but not. My brain felt numbingly, painfully compressed in my little skull but also nonexistent like reading a blank paper. I guess I was walking, I'm not really sure how. I mean ya, one foot in front of another; but I don't feel it. I see it, but I don't feel it. My sight and touch conflicted and clashing heads, but I didn't seem to care. All my senses weren't my own, but instead I belonged to them. My brain is rambling, but not talking at all. A million words squeezing my brain is just like a gust of air into an empty balloon. I feel the tingling sensation of tension in my hand. Grasping onto something. I can't put my finger on what it is; just something I need. How did I get my hands on it? I don't know. I don't even know where my hands, arms, or limbs are. Because of my proprioception's abandonment, I can't describe every moment or feeling or sensation without using my mind to fill in the blanks that I just didn't experience in the moment.

I can't look at what is in my hand.

I can't make myself stop walking.

I can't stop my body from moving.

I don't even know what my body wants me to do. My head and my body are of their own will, and I feel like I've lost control of both. I am watching myself walk out the door. I'm in my body, in my head, and also watching from a third party perspective at myself grab the door knob and turn it without feeling any feeling in my body or mind.

Where am I? Looking at the time. I'm in my car. In a parking lot. In the parking lot of a Jack in the Box. It's been an hour. 14 notifications. 14 calls, 14 voicemail messages. Each one describing the fact that the person who was trying to contact me had been trying to contact me for an hour straight to make sure I was okay. I drove away from home and was driving for a solid hour. I didn't remember any of it, or even feel anything at all.

I have several mental illnesses and I have experienced many intense experiences of dissociation and derealization. I have never understood it, but find myself constantly thinking I've gone insane because, apparently, I can drive for an hour without remembering any of it and without causing myself to crash. It starts out like a feeling of being in a haze and in a dream. I can't speak, I can't do anything that my head wants me to do, but my body seems to have a mind of its own; all while I'm watching myself do all of these things. It is the scariest feeling in the world and I feel alone and insane.

I don't have a diagnosed disorder for dissociative identities, but I did end up getting really intrigued by the developed neurological disorder when watching one Youtuber in particular: DissociaDID.

I watched a video where Nin, one of the alters of DissociaDID, stated, "as a child, your personality was unable to fully develop into one singular personality. Everybody as a child starts off with an unintegrated personality, and around the ages between 7-9 in normal development. But if there is repeated or severe trauma before that age..." (quoted from an Anthony Padilla video featuring Nin in one portion) the brain finds a way to cope which could alternatively turn to forming alternative identities to survive that trauma. DID, or Dissociative Identity Disorder, is a sort of coping mechanism that is trauma based. In other words, DID is a neurological disorder where identities are formed from dissociating and amnesia wall going up for long periods of time. The formation of "alters" is a coping with the trauma through memory loss in order to stimulate the most "normal" life possible to survive. Dissociative Identity Disorder is a developed disorder, and oftentimes stems from a young age. The normal final development of a person's personality happens around the ages of 7-9; but if there is a trauma before that age, they have high levels of dissociation from birth, and they have a disorganized attachment to their caregivers; developing DID is high. The response to these things is that your brain will dissociate as much as possible, which can end up causing the formation of different alters to cope with the different experiences or traumas presented at such a young age. There are many different types of dissociative disorders, so I highly recommend doing some research on the non-well known topic with millions of stigmas surrounding it from the media.

I did research on the topic because I personally felt interested in several things I watched about DID and felt a certain level of connection to the phenomenon. It is a disorder different for everyone who experiences it, because it is a very personal disorder. To add to that, the disorder is formulated from personal severe trauma that is always going to be different from everyone and also everyone's coping mechanisms are specified to each person. I do not have DID, and I am very blessed and humbled by that fact. However, I have personally experienced moments of disconnection because of my childhood traumas, mental health instability, a lack of a strong parental system, and trauma from the constant feelings of pain and hurt that automatically associates with my family in my mind. Some are more intense than others, and sometimes it takes a larger toll on me to feel like I can't even keep myself from dissociating and running away in my own mind. Am I weak? Is that just me running and fleeing from my problems?

I hated myself for it, because I blamed myself for this subconscious black out of my memories. But is it really my fault? Developmentally, I have always repressed memories as a defense mechanism to the hard, trauma inducing times in my life. Often it was a result of childhood trauma triggers that I am unaware of due to memory loss.

Honor thy father and thy mother. I believe that I love my family with my whole heart and I am most lenient to do things for them for their benefit over mine, but at times it gets to be overwhelming. I overwork myself to please them and overwork myself to try to get some sort of reciprocation of the love i'm projecting to get nothing; as a result, my memories simply get marked out in black leaving behind a form with only the words 'why is there pain in love' left on the page surrounded by darkness.

Chapter 30

ME EM

S kin like the shimmering surface of the pool on a summer day, she stood across from me. Confronting each other, looking at each other through a crystal clear piece of glass. Hairless arms crossed and slouched over the counter, just staring. She was wearing a skirt that didn't exactly fit, but she looked great. Me, on the other hand, not so much. Looking down, I can just see and feel my stomach rolling over the hem at my waist. Sucking in and no matter how much I turned her legs or flexed my stomach, it still looked bad. Her blouse fit nicely and pushed up her breasts in a flattering way; while when I try to pull off that same exact top, I look unsettlingly lacking in aesthetic proportion. I wish I could just wrap my chest compactly into my chest to relieve myself of the burden of trying to make them look 'just right'. I just couldn't get it to that point.

I mean I guess I *like* who I am. I guess I can *cope* with who I am, I can *deal* with it. But if you were to ask me what my favorite accomplishment has been, the favorite thing about myself, the one quality about me that I absolutely adore I would never trade for anything else; I wouldn't be able to give you an answer. Don't get me wrong, I'm proud of how far I've gone. I'm proud of who I am. I can carry myself around confidently. But none of that comes from a place of adoring who I am as a person. None of that comes from self-love, sadly. Are you even at least slightly curious about where it comes from? Well, the answer is clear: *insecurity.*

Why is it that whenever anyone mentions the word *'insecurity'* everyone freaks out? The truth of the matter is that a majority of the things about ourselves comes from a place of insecurity. Bending in every shape, *angle*, and every geOmeTRic pOsSibILIty that comes into our imaginations of what our bodies look best like. I mean it's *one* rib, no big deal. Opening every single textbook you can get your paws on, just to remember one page of one textbook. Taking every single test prep opportunity, just to get an average score. Biting your tongue trying not to scream, for every step, the heel digs in. The heel of your shoe constantly poking, but you move forward. The insecurities about our **bodies**, our **brains**, and our **personalities** drive us to become the people we are and do the things we do.

I'm not a confident person at heart. I'm not the smartest in the room. I'm not the most artistic in the room. And I most definitely not the person who loves herself the most in any room. The way I act around different people, the way I bring myself about the world to bring positivity, the way I am; all of it I don't know if it's a lie. A facade to try to cover up the insecurity. Every insecurity is valid, but no one is *that* good at pretending. Or I sure hope not. She sure wasn't pretending. she didn't seem to have to. She didn't have any insecurities.

She is so pretty. She didn't have to try, it was natural. I mean just a simple smile and everyone sees her confidence and her happiness. While me, well, I just don't project that energy. I'm the exact opposite. I project hatred for the world, a sense of resentment for myself transferring to those around me, the energy of judgment that can only drive others away, and an energy that I don't even want to be around.

Looking at the clear glass, I lifted my hand and she mocked me. I placed my hand upon the mirror and felt the cold touch of reality.

I realized she was *me.*

Like in a daze, I couldn't look away. I felt paralyzed looking into my own gaze, like the girl in the mirror had reached through the reflection to grab me. She looked so sweet, but at this moment, she felt like a shadow of what I had hoped to be but could never be. A taunt. I genuinely thought the girl in the mirror was someone different. Someone who I felt proud of. At the start, someone I could feel so happy for but now has become a sense of disdain. I distanced myself and disassociated myself with myself. *Gosh.*

Labored breathing left my body, as I looked directly into her eyes, and she continued to smile. A tear dripped from my eyes and I watched as she revealed she also was in pain. The happiness and content I had once seen in her revealed itself to be a charade. A pain that I didn't notice before. She was broken inside.

Letting my hand outline her face, she seemed terrified at the concept of me stroking her face to comfort her. Was it the action of touching her that scared her? Or the feeling that someone pitied her? Or could it just be she was scared of the comfort? Eventually, she rested her head in my hand, and I looked at her, my heart hurting and swelling for her pain. I wish I could help her, and I wish that other people knew.

I'm scared. I need to get out of this dissociation, something about this feels all eerie and I feel like someone is watching me. Maybe it was just the girl in the mirror, but I really didn't like the feeling.

"Let me out! Let me be, okay?!" she screamed through the glass.

My heart dropped, and I tried to grab her hand in mine, but all she could manage was to touch my fingertips. Her fingers cold, her heart icing over and cracking, ready to shatter. *I'm sorry.*

Closing my eyes to cry, I drew back into the daze and dissociation. I couldn't grasp the reality quite yet, I wanted to, but couldn't. It all felt unresolved. I felt myself drawback even more. The next thing I knew, I felt myself watching the older version of myself still stuck in the internal battle with her reflection. I had reached a further point of dissociation I didn't realize I could reach. I was watching myself from a third-person struggling to manage her dissociation from her own reflection. But this time, I was paralyzed. I was watching from her left and I couldn't reach out to comfort her. She couldn't hear me. I was a ghost, without a voice. I screamed. I cried. But she stayed sitting there in front of the mirror with her gaze upon the other girl in the mirror.

Three people with three times the pain.

All three girls closed their eyes at the same time and focused so hard on wanting to escape this maze of my mind, I dropped to the ground and stared at the ceiling as one being again. Paralyzed, I layed there for a while confused, terrified, horrified, and scared of the eerie feeling of being possessed by inner demons that dissociation took hold of my body.

Chapter 31

DISORDER

What do you qualify as a disorder?

According to psychology, a disorder is when a state of being causes harm to yourself and/or to your society you reside in. Unless it causes harm to yourself or others, it's just a quirk.

I keep going back.

I don't want to. I just do.

There are those days when my body and my mind work together to betray me, dragging me back. Back to that house, back to that room, back to that bed, back to that shower, back to that feeling. The physical and mental feeling. All of it. Just rushes back.

Waking up in the morning, and the first thing that happens is that my vision seems to blur and my skin crawls. My whole body paralyzes with a minimal chill shaking my nerves. My sight is blurred from reality, but I can clearly see it. I'm back. I'm being raped. Right now.

I can't breathe. My fists clench and my jaw clenches as my throat seems to close. I'm powerless, and back there. Another flash, and I'm back to reality trying to recover. Finally breathing like I just came straight out of water. And I get up to try to move on from the flashback and then trauma.

I'm at school, in my first block. My teacher is talking but I'm not listening. I'm so tired. I've seen the flashback twice again in class already. I want a break. *Please.* No. I'm back there once again without breathing. Choking, on nothing but my mind. Like my soul goes back there but leaves my body in the place it is.

And Once again.

And again.

And again.

Again.

Once more.

And more.

More.

It never ends.

I keep going back.

Getting rushed back.

Flashes in my eyes.

Trauma spreading through my whole being.

I think this is what they call

PTSD, a disorder.

Chapter 32

COAL TO DIAMONDS

Nobody is perfect. In fact, almost everyone has some kind of mental illness, maybe not disorder, but illness. And some of us seek help and get it, but are marked forever.

My baby bird had a few feathers plucked. Looking at her, you can see a few of her feathers losing their color, less vibrant. She has had a journey she has had to survive through, and I knew. She didn't have to tell me, I could see it in her eyes. In her soul.

"What is your biggest pet peeve?" We were playing a game of the Question Game on the bus back to Dallas from ISAS. Erial asked Jean.

"Ummm…"

"Literally anything."

"Ummm… I guess when people say, 'I just want to die' just to be dramatic. It bothers me because I know what it feels like to want to die because of my depression and after I have in the past felt like that, it bothers me when people use it to just be dramatic when there are people who do want to actually die." *A solid answer, and one I never thought about but understand. I don't say that but that is good to know.*

"Oh My God. I say that all the time!"...*Why did Erial think that was necessary to say? Why is she like this?*

"I understand, and I respect that. I never thought of it like that, and that is some really good insight. I bet you aren't the only one who feels that way. I don't think I do that often but I'll be more cautious of it. Also, I am very glad that that is something that is in your past and you've grown from it, that is very commendable," I put in my piece.

"Thank you." Jean's facial expression changed to a more calm one after the one of confusion to Erial's remark.

Our lives have changed quite a bit since then. After ISAS, I came back home to my life with my family and my problems, and it started to eat at me. Jean left Erial's friendship and instantly became my friend when we came back and mostly just followed me. It was nice, I suppose, but I didn't really open up much. But she began to, to me. Because unlike Erial, I listened to her and gave her some insight to help her feel better. But it was a lot for me. It began to pile up. All of it. And soon, I finally opened up to her.

Ever heard of how if you put a lot of pressure on coal, you will get a diamond? Don't fact check that though, because it isn't true. But for the sake of this, let's say it is. The pressures of the world, and the pressures of the things I held myself responsible for, I simply hoped one day I would emerge a diamond. One day. In the meantime, Jean stood strong next to me as the pressure of the world pressed us against ourselves.

Jean opened up about her depression and her anxiety. She opened up about her mental health and mental state. Sometimes more unstable than other times. And I soon found myself realizing that there are moments of relating to her. The scientific and logical side of me would analyze that to come out with the analysis of my understanding of my own mental health. It would say I was depressed. *But there was no way. No way. I wasn't. I could be a diamond, I was just a little rusty. I wasn't depressed though. No. I was not.*

Chapter 33

ALL KNOWING

I don't know where anyone is. I think Jean is off to do some spanish project. Bailey is with her boyfriend in the music room. And everyone is sorta gone. I guess I will go sit in the area we usually hang out and see if anyone was there. I sat on the coach facing the window and watched through the reflection of the glass who was coming and going through the hall behind me and to the side of me. The friend group was there but they were leaving to go hang out in another room while eating lunch.

"Hey, Dew Itty, are you coming?"

"No, I'm good," a hesitant smile.

I know that look. I've worn that look. We weren't close, and I honestly haven't talked to him one-on-one ever. But, he was not okay. I heard that recently that his girlfriend had broken up with him. It was inevitable because she had gone to college, but still. It must have been hard. I bet that was what it was. I think he might be really depressed. Almost... suicidal.

The guys left and I sat there with Dew Itty alone. His eyes sucked and concentrated on his computer screen, clearly trying to focus on anything other than his feelings.

"Hey, I have a question," suddenly I spoke.

He looked up at me and responded, "Sure, what's up?"

"I want an honest answer and I know it is a kind of weird question. I know we aren't close but I was just curious cause I noticed."

"What, dummy? Just ask bruh." Dew Itty was known for coming off as a bit harsh when it came to his speech, so I knew that this meant he was opening up a bit and not fully in his head anymore.

"I was just wondering if everything is okay with you and the guys?"

"Ya, what the fuck? We are fine. Why?"

"I don't know, I sort of just have noticed you've been alone more often than you are with them. And that seems unordinary. They also didn't seem to want to ask you to come with them. Like they didn't seem to want to push you to come and join like they used to."

"Ya, ummm... I guess when I was dating Lina, she sort of calmed down my personality a bit; but now that we are broken up, the guys aren't as used to my big personality anymore. And they aren't as used to me being as loud anymore." *That wasn't the whole truth, but that's okay. Maybe he doesn't know, and he doesn't want to figure it out. I know him though because we've been in the same friend group for so long. He doesn't know me, but I know him. What he needs, is to feel useful. Without a girlfriend, he has lost his purpose. I will give him a new one.*

"Oh, I see. Well, you know they love you. They loved you before you dated Lina and they will love you now. But I get not wanting to impose that upon them... but I was wondering, could I get your advice on something?"

"Of course. What's up?"

"Um, I've been having some issues with my family. I haven't told anyone about it. I haven't even told Jean or Bailey, because I don't know. I haven't really been able to talk about it."

"What's wrong?"

"My mom told me that she doesn't love my dad anymore and she might not be straight. She might like women. But, I will accept her for whatever she identifies no matter what. I love her. The problem is now I have had to lie to my dad. I can't tell him. My life just has been full of lies and deceit. I don't know what to do. What should I do?"

He was invested. It worked! His body language changed and he got up to sit closer to me as he tried to comfort me and give me advice. I was considering pulling the full stop to crying, but crying is hard. So I didn't.

Instantly, he started to feel more comfortable with me. He opened up to me and started talking to me about how he honestly had not been doing well mentally. How he was suicidal. And I didn't lie. "I knew."

"You knew?! How did you know?"

"I just... knew."

"Wait. Is that why you talked to me? Is that why?" *I knew he needed honesty so I didn't lie.*

"Yes. But, I didn't want to make you feel obligated to tell me anything. I just want you to know you have something to live for. If I can make it through my shit, you can too, right?"

"Ya, I guess," a genuine smile now.

"You are kind of all knowing, aren't you?" We both genuinely laughed.

And that was how I got my best friend. Someone to keep me alive and someone I keep alive everyday.

Chapter 34

PERSPECTIVE

If you really think about it, it's all about perspective. Our outlooks may be similar because we experience the same situation, but we still don't experience the same thing; this is because of *perspective*. I walk into a room with you, but what I analyze and what I see will always be different from what you do. We both look at the same person, but we interpret whether or not they're good for us or bad for us in different ways. I may be their friend, while you aren't, or vice versa. Our judgment is different because our *perspective* is different. Surprisingly, we're friends, but how we view our friendship is different.

*   *   *

hey.

This is hard for me to say, so bear with me. Please.

As you know, I've never felt a true understanding of emotions. I am at a constant tie between feeling overwhelmed by a whirlwind of emotions or distinctly lacking the emotions to express or divulge into. I used to think of myself as an intellectual computer, an input, and output sort of person; ignoring the process in between.

I was wrong, and I have grown to learn that it is okay that I was wrong. I'm ready to learn to open up a bit more about the understanding that I wasn't deprived of emotions, I was just numbingly defending myself from the overwhelming number of emotions plausible for me to experience. To you, this may seem strange, or you may think that I am overreacting and naive for ever thinking I could simply just not have emotions. But I sure hope you don't judge me. I am writing to you, and I hope you realize how much of a risk I am taking in doing so because so much can be lost in translation. *Will you respond properly? Will you leave me? Will I lose another?* I hope my judgment is correct *this* time. I hope I wasn't wrong to do this. I guess I can only hope.

There is a lot of my life you don't know. To you, you definitely don't find this weird. You and I both know it is because I am a private person, am not too adamant about speaking to my emotions, and we just aren't that close. Not many people know we are close, not many people know we facetime almost every other day, not many people know you come to me when you need help; all simply because that is what friends do. I'm nothing too special, just one of many of your friends; and never your top choice. If we hang out, it is one on one or with a mutual friend; but never with your usual friends. I don't fit, and you act differently between the two so why mix them. Because that is what friends do. That's your perspective. *Arm's length.*

Switching lenses, looking at our friendship from another view; my heart is revealed. I can't tell you. I can't let you in. "How's everything?" you ask me. I relent a snit-bit, an update of sorts. It lacks the authenticity of emotion and cannot be divulged into. I'm closed off, because... I can't. I feel useful when I'm with you, in a way that I need. In a way, that keeps my heart beating. I became friends with you at first to learn to be a bit more human. I wanted to learn to interact with others, I wanted to learn how people show they care, I wanted to learn how to enjoy a life unlived, and I wanted to laugh. That's it. Just laugh. And you did make me laugh. You make me laugh still. But now, you come to me with your concerns. You come to me with your troubles. You come to the being that won't develop feelings for you but feels for you in a way no one else will, because I see you.

I know you well enough to know your true intentions. *How would I describe our friendship?* Well to start...

True. The world has turned its back on you more than once. I have always been someone who has resided in the bottom half of the social hierarchy by choice. Taking a skill test for a leadership thing we both did for a class, one of my skills was inclusion. For my specific form of inclusion though, I purposefully exclude myself from the general group to join the person who is isolated outside the clique to make them feel included with me. It has never bothered me to think that my friendships fluctuate and that I will never stay in one place with one group forever. But you are different. You have to have a circle/ group of friends as a constant. Most people are this way. The usual support group, the group that is there for you through thick and thin, and the group that makes you feel confident in your flaws. A level of validation comes from this form of friendship, I admire it. I have never had that, and I have never felt the need of other people; this is my flaw. Without the need of other people, I leave before I get hurt. I leave to help someone else and leave behind others to feel neglected. You would never. You mingle, you jump from group to group to make everyone feel included; but you ultimately return to your place in the social pyramid, the top. You used to occasionally interact with me to let me feel included, but I knew I was just another person out of the many you talk to. You don't truly see me for me, but I can see you. Sophomore year struck you down from your cloud 9, and you came down to meet me. Your friends all turned their backs on you because of a measly rumor that passed around. One that only the one with true eyes could see was clearly a lie smudging others' perception of you. It was unfair. It was heart-wrenching for me to watch. I heard the rumor in passing and immediately spotted the lie. I knew you, and your friends should too. I thought that undeniably your friends should know that to be so too. Whoever believes it to be true clearly never saw you or understood you. With inevitable descension, you became lonely and consumed by the unworthy feeling and being unrightfully placed into this cruel stopping point. You couldn't do anything about it. I approached you, and you knew that I knew. You knew I knew the rumors weren't true. You knew that I knew *you*. I helped you through that rut and was so happy to watch you grow from it. You have your ups and downs obviously, but I am always here. You don't always need my aid, so we stopped talking for long periods of time after that incident, but that just gave me proof of the result. You made friends again, and no longer needed me as often; meaning I did help you. *True.* I say that our friendship is true, because I know you would never lie to me, and I know you. I see you. I see you for who you are, who you want to be, and who you are to me: my friend. The journey we've been through has been one that was hard on you. But you stuck with it. You pushed through it with moments of hesitancy but you still did it. You are a true person. A true person who is willing to fight for the right to be human. Fight for the right to stay who you are despite what others say about you. To fight to get the rightful friends that care for you without changing yourself to comply with others and give in to their hearsay. You are true, and as a result, you have made our friendship so as well.

Lenient. I am lenient with you because I care about you. You probably don't know this, but I let a lot of things that you say that could be taken offensively go. You can sometimes say some sexist or racist comment, and I let it go. You think something that is just wrong is funny, and I laugh at the understanding that in a certain lens it is funny. You almost never call me to just talk or want to hang out with me just because you enjoy my company, but that's okay. When you speak to me often you just talk to me like a soundboard, and I have accepted it. You ask me to help you with something, and every instinct in my body screams that I don't want to, but I do it. At times you ask me to do things for you, and I do it to the best of my ability. I give it a shot, despite wanting to just not. I am lenient with you because I let you feel confident in who you are and let you feel like maybe, just maybe, though the world often says otherwise, you are worthy. You are special. You deserve the world. I want you to feel like you could reach your cloud 9 again, though it will never be the same. I do what I can because I care about you. I do what I can because... I am your friend. I don't make promises I can't keep and I claim to be something I can't pull through on. When I became your friend, I will keep stick to it. I will stick with you, especially when you ask me to.

Life-worthy. Worthwhile to put it in the simplest form possible. I don't think I deserve you, I don't think that I am qualified to be that person for you when you need help, I don't think I am that special of a person in any way to be worth any of your time, and I don't think that I am worthy of being your friend. But *you. You* are worth every second of anyone's time. You turn heads as you enter a room and everyone hypes you up. Everyone should be there for you when you need help, everyone should wish to be your friend, and everyone should see you for who you are without any hesitation as to what your true intentions are. Maybe I'm overexaggerating how great you are. You are human to be fair. You have many flaws and to your face I point every single one. Messing with you on how you can not cut a paper straight with a drawn line. Picking at you for every photo taken of you by the school yearbook that makes you look like a dufus. Laughing and joking about how you can't seem to kickstart your love life, liking so many girls with a lot of potential but something gets in the way. I make fun of you for your flaws but you know that I have so much respect for you. You make my life so entertaining, help me laugh authentically. You make my life worthwhile. You are life-worthy.

Equally Unequal. We are equals... sort of. You seem to view us on a certain level equally, where we are above others and can talk about how the rest of the world is wrong or incompetant. Do I always agree? No. I have never indulged in the 'incompetence' of others. I believe that when I don't agree with other people or they are doing things I would never do myself, I ignore it. I think that people won't listen to me even if I suggested they take another approach; people are stubborn and won't learn unless they learn on their own. So, though I know most things going on by observing, I let life go the way it will go. You, on the other hand, can't leave it alone. Seeing something that bothers you, you come to me or another one of your friends and make it a point to state that their actions are 'incompetant'. Have I ever been 'incompetant'? I suppose not, and that is why you view us as equals. I don't think that I am good enough to be considered your equal, but I think that just speaks to my depression, self-confidence issues, trust issues, and etc. That seems beside the point.

Intellectual. Without a doubt, you are an intellectual. When you approach anything in your life, you are strategic and avoid emotional connection as much as possible to reduce the chance of being vulnerable. You want to be productive, not stuck in you 'feels'. I suppose that is why when the incident with your friends hit so close to home for you. It hurt you so much because you had no choice but to face your emotions without portraying 'emotional'. I hate saying anything about my emotions. I hate expressing any sense of vulnerability, but I do do it at times to give off the illusion that I am willing to be vulnerable with someone to create rapport and trust. But would I consider myself 'emotional'? No. By no means. I am an intellectual who can manipulate my words, my actions, and can strategically manage to get away with not being vulnerable while being vulnerable. I am an intellectual who seeks productivity in relationships because that was always my weak suit. We are two intellectuals who keep up with the news of the world and keep up with the productivity of our lives. We seek to grow and seek to succeed, and can speak to each other about topics in a productive manner and in a manner that allows us to judiciously feed off of each other.

Useful. This one is mostly for me. I can't speak to your perspective, and I can't speak as to whether I have actually been of any importance to your life. At times it feels as if I am a speck of dust in the pile of things you want to manage. I am one of many, with little importance but still important. To me our friendship is useful for me. I have had many moments of self-doubt, moments of loss, and moments of depression. I have a constant feeling of finding my life has no meaning, my life is one of unimportance, and my life has no permanence in the world for anyone. Because of this cognitive way of thinking, I have found myself sucked into my suicidal thoughts and depressive spirals. But I needed a distraction. I needed a sense of usefulness and purpose for my life, or at least an excuse to continue onward. Though I felt horrible and felt my heart tear when you had to go through any sense of hardship in your life and I was there; I have to shamefully admit that I prospered on a level from it. I felt useful to someone's life when I helped you. I didn't think I was doing much, but I felt a purpose to continue on and not give up on you halfway like others did. I wanted to see you through the dark to the other end. It made me want to live. And, on rare occasions, you would show some appreciation. It was rare, but it was there. I felt like maybe, just maybe, my cryptic brain was wrong. Maybe, I have a reason to live. Maybe, I am useful. Maybe, just maybe, I should keep trying.

Love. I love you with my whole heart. When you cry, my heart weeps. When you grow, my heart beats. When you are you, my heart sings to the tune you skip down your path towards your future. I feel for you so much, and you are one of my closest friends. I may not be one of yours, but you definitely are one of mine without a doubt. I hate to admit this in person because I fend from any form of vulnerability, but our friendship does matter to me.

Our perspectives may be different on our friendship, but I sure hope we both feel the same way when it comes to this... I love you so much, so much more than I think you can understand; and I regret nothing about the time that our paths have crossed. I love you, Nadim. Thank you.

Always your friend,
Wynn Thành Phi

Chapter 35

JIMINY CRICKET'S COURTROOM

I t is apparently normal to have an internal voice that is telling you what is right or wrong. A *Jiminy Cricket* if you will.

Jiminy Cricket represented the inner conscience working in the mind of an innocent boy new to the world. Pinnochio, similar to an infant, was brought into a world believing everything he heard due to the lack of experience and in need of direction. The Blue Fairy, a parallel to G*d or superior power that grants wishes of those of pure intentions and good at heart, grants Gepetto's wish. The Blue Fairy offers Pinocchio a life of choices and free will, just as G*d did for His people. Pinocchio had to prove himself to be a 'good person' essentially in order to fulfill his destiny as a real boy. As soon as this arrangement is made, alluding to the concept of G*d's ten commandments that would bring good fortune, the Blue Fairy essentially gave Pinocchio a choice: become a real boy and receive a sort of "spiritual salvation" through "self-discipline, self-knowledge and intense will power" or have the gifts given to you get taken away. The blue fairy grants the puppet a conscience, which brings up a new concept. This conscience was Jiminy Cricket. This very adorable character is made to personify the perfect conscience, which does not exist; according to ohmy.disney.com, Jiminy Cricket is a "Lord High Keeper of the knowledge of right and wrong, counselor in moments of temptation, and guide along the straight and narrow path". But in a Freudian view, 'Jiminy Cricket' would be your superego, your mortality compass of your personality residing in your unconscious.

We each have a Jiminy Cricket of our own. Each one is different because realistically, it is formed due to experience and understanding of learning morality. However, everyone's understanding of morality is different.

Looking from side to side, checking to see if there is risk, reward, or realization of the consequences; you take the leap. You go across the street, entering the green. A new world of wonder and exhilaration. You are trespassing onto the lands of the private property clearly labeled. Where was your Jiminy Cricket then? He was there. He was watching you. But your demons pushed him aside. But if you listen carefully, can you hear him?

By any chance did he say something along the lines of, "You're going to get in trouble, don't do it". Or was it more like, "this is wrong, you know this isn't right, go back". There are different levels of morality ranging from doing things based on whether you think there is a chance of getting caught and getting in trouble to simply knowing it is right or wrong. Some people sit and balance out the risks and positive outcomes to see the end result justify the means. Morality is fluid and abstract, though often forced to conform to a single black and white view on life. We like to simplify the necessity of having a conscience by honing it down to a singular character, a singular voice. But in reality, we all have a small little council in our heads. But whether that council works in your favor every situation is entirely dependent on you as an individual.

Playing judge, jury, counsel, and victim; my mind takes the role of many. You could even say I am adaptable that way, to be able to survive in any role. Walking into the room, my mind betrays me. Often, you may hear an often depressed notion is that it is when you feel like your mind is betraying you and hurting you instead of assisting you.

"She hates you."

> *"No, she doesn't, she loves you. She is your friend."*
> *"She is acting that way to be nice."*

"She really just hates you. No other explanation."

> *"She cares about you. You are just overthinking."*
> *"Maybe... but I am still not deserving of it"*

"You are deserving of it."

> *"Not from her."*

"If you can't even love yourself, how can you expect someone else to?"

"If you can't even think you deserve it..."

> *"...You can't ask for it from someone else..."*
> *"... it isn't fair..."*

"You are undeserving of love, so even if she does care, she can't love you. It isn't fair of you to even possibly think she does and it isn't fair for you to think you are worth it. It isn't fair of you to hypocritically expect her to, when you can't love yourself. Shut up. Just shut the f*ck up and die."

"Die."

> *"Die."*

"Die."

Final Ruling: Guilty of being *Unlovable*. Sentenced to Death by Lethal Injection of Internal Turmoil.

Chapter 36

NO, I'M IN CONTROL

Dew itty looked at me and asked, "Are you okay?"

That's a loaded question. *'Are'* is a to-be verb, showing a state of being. A state of being that you equal, something that defines you as a person or an object. Oftentimes frowned upon in writing, to be verbs establish a sense of definition that can either be permanent or temporary, but it's a promise to be as you state. A cage, a limitation, and a claim of being something. *'You'* is a pronoun, referring to a person directly. In other words a calling out or a calling to. A term used to make it more personal, for the good or for the bad. A calling out to tell you that you can't run away from this accusation, this claim, this limitation, this cage. *'Okay'*, the worst of this whole question. A broken promise to be okay. I can't even define the term. It isn't a form of being in a state of being normal. It is *'abstract'* as I've been told. So how can you be called out to promise to be in a state of being something you never understood?

"I'm okay," I suppose this is true, but should I mention *it?*

"To be honest, I do need to get something off of my chest," *will I say?*

"Ok, what's up?"

It started a few weeks ago at most; I started to feel like my life was slipping through my fingers. Like I had a loss of control and all I wanted to do was squeeze my skin off of my body like an orange peel, reveling in the possibility that such a physical, violent act can relent me of my mental and emotional weight.

"Nevermind."

"No, really. What's wrong?"

I felt my fingernails gauge into my sides and I felt like I was trapped in my estranged arms. I wasn't hugging myself, I was strangling myself. I wasn't comforting myself, I was killing myself.

"It's nothing, don't worry about it."

"Hey, you're starting to worry me. Why can't you tell me? What's wrong?"

I wanted to clench onto my body and rip off every last piece of the quilt, revealing just the fraying of the thread. I wanted to throw myself in the trash like I threw away that dried up, rotten banana I just looked at and felt disgusted. I grabbed it this morning, actually for breakfast. At first, I thought I'd enjoy it; but the thought of what my brain associated it with could not seem to be ridden from my mind.

"I figured it out, Nevermind."

"You're lying. Just tell me, you can trust me."

I am a plastic bag drifting through the wind wanting to start again and not end up choking off a poor innocent animal that deserved to live. I want to change who I am.

"No, really. I figured it out," I smiled *meekly*.

"Are you sure?"

"Yes," *Lie* through my teeth.

"I don't believe you," Dew Itty didn't buy it for a minute.

Dew Itty had been prompting me for the whole lunch block in the lounge at school we usually hang out in. It was an arrangement of blue couches facing a central rectangular table, shorter than seat cushions. I always took a seat on the couch closest to the window, or I took the seat across from them. That way, I had a perfect view of all the hallways and all my surroundings. From the seat against the windows, I could look freely outward; while, from the seat facing the windows, my back faced one of the hallways, but my view was not obstructed but reflected upon the windows. I had to be in control and see everything. I can see anyone coming up the hall and I can make notes and analyze every single action of those who passed by.

Most days, I'd skip lunch, and just stay upstairs in the lounge and take a moment to breathe. I often had one earbud in, listening to music, and Dew Itty became accustomed to staying there with me. Jean was there too usually, but I assumed she was busy with some other meeting today. Therefore, I was put on the spot.

In all honesty, I wasn't okay. I continued to press upon myself and reassure myself otherwise though. Looking straight at Dew Itty, I just saw pity and remorse. I don't need that. Don't do that. I knew he was trying to do what was best for me; but, *really*, I was managing. I am handling everything, but everything felt out of control, everything was falling apart.

My family situation wasn't getting any better; in fact, it felt like it escalated to a new level of crumbling. I barely saw my mother, I assumed she was either at work, at the hospital getting checkups, at the hospital working out, or, for all I know, with her friend. She didn't tell me anything anymore, only once in a while. And those few moments would always occur in the car when I was with her alone and moving in the same direction without making eye-contact. It was the only way we could talk honestly. She would pour her heart out about enjoyable times she was having with her friend, or about moments that she regrets in informing me of the truth. She had regret for involving me in something I should never have had to worry about. She had her *own* sense of guilt. And I understood, but the responsibility I feel is one of my own. It has nothing to do with her, she was just being human. I could never blame her for anything.

I love her.

My sister, on the other hand, will talk to me every day. She had no sense of stopping, and I had always been there to listen to her in the past. Any moment she had concerns or had menial drama she couldn't sort out, I would listen and provide insight. This was no different. She would tell me about how her friends don't have to go through what we have to go through, and it wasn't fair. She didn't understand why we couldn't just keep on living as a happy family. But we never wore one. At the time she didn't see this, so I continue to sit through her melodrama and her feelings of the unfairness of the world. The way that a naïve child would believe that something could actually be perfect in this imperfect world, she had that still. I never want her to lose that. *Honestly.* I lost that ages ago, even before I knew that it should be treasured.

I can't even look at him. I can't acknowledge anything. He acts so normally, nothing happened. There's no way anything happened. He couldn't be that normal about it if something did. It is definitely in my head. Just be normal with him. I continue to talk to my dad like nothing ever happened. I was still there for him, he called me his best friend, and he believed, genuinely, I was his only friend and the only person who loved or cared about him. He loved me, right? He was my dad, he'd never do anything to hurt me. He cared about me and was proud of me, and needed me. He would never do anything to hurt me, at least not on purpose. It was just in my head. I thought it up. It was my fault. Or, if I didn't make it up, and all that happened really happened, then he had good reason. He didn't feel loved. My mom didn't love him, they slept separately ever since I was born, and it was my fault. I couldn't fix it, and I was the last good thing to happen for their marriage. It was me, who ended it all. I had to be there for him because he needed someone. And no one else would be there for him. It was my fault, I'll hold accountability. Someone has to. I'll listen to him complain, whine, and even curse about how his life is unfair. About how his life fell apart. About how the only reason my mom stayed around was because of me and my sister. The only reason my mom married my dad was to have kids. About every little heartache, I was there to *listen*.

I was managing. I *really* was. I was holding myself responsible for the things that I was responsible for. My family needed me, and that's more important than anything else. I felt exhausted, even disgusted with myself because of the pain that was happening in my inner soul that I felt ashamed of. The priority of my family trumped my school work, and it consumed me fully. Every thought went to trying to keep sane. Hearing every perspective, while still remaining calm and not stabbing anyone in the back by sharing the secret with another member of the family. At school, it followed me in the halls; I could feel the chains binding me to home.

> "Wynn?" Dew Itty looked at me eagerly, as I regained consciousness to reality, "I think you have depression, like actually. I have depression, and I used to get help for it. I think you should."

His intent was honest and true, but I knew the truth, "I can't."

"Why?"

> "Because, Dew Itty, my parents don't believe in mental health issues, they don't even know what's wrong. You don't. Or at least not all of it. And I don't plan on asking to get help if I can't even bring myself to tell them something. How can I tell a complete stranger something if I can't tell my parents or my loved ones?"

My parents were brought up in a more traditional lifestyle, where success was determined by money and mental health was a dismissable thing that didn't exist. You just had to push through it, because they would have. They wouldn't even be struggling with this kind of thing, they would have gutted it and moved on to better days. So why can't I? If they knew I was struggling this much, they'd truly be disappointed in what I had become.

> "Wynn. Really. I think you need help. I know I don't know everything because you are like a locked box with the key inside. There is no way I can make you take down ALL of your walls, I honestly feel privileged enough for you to allow me to help a little and let me in a little. But really, I think you should try to get some professional help," that look of pity again.

"No, there is nothing wrong with me. I am perfectly fine. I'm managing. No, I'm in control. Anyone in my shoes would be fine and I am fine."

"Ok, how about this, as a compromise, you go see Dr. Murial?"

Dr. Murial was the school counselor. She was there as a resource for students to come in and talk to her if they ever felt any toll in their life or just needed to talk. She was basically a therapist in the office around the other corner who could honestly hear every conversation you have, and pull you in if she heard anything of "concern". She was a kind woman, but honestly, every time I saw her I got paranoid. It wasn't because of who she was or her personality, but it was because of what she represented. Going in to talk to Dr. Murial would be like accepting defeat, it would be like accepting I wasn't doing fine on my own. I wasn't managing. But I was. *Really.* Also, going in to see her, and telling her these secrets of mine could ruin everything. It could jeopardize my future in seeing the events that had happened to me, it could jeopardize my relationship with my parents, it could jeopardize *everything.* It is unsafe to allow anyone else on my secret; it wouldn't bring anything positive whatsoever. Also, going in to see a school counselor, in my mind, had a stigma of marking me as crazy or weak. I just couldn't accept that. If anyone else went in to see her, it didn't mean that; but for me, I would hate myself for it. I just *know* I would.

"Wynn, before you scoff at it and turn away, which I know you already doing," *it is funny how he knows me so well,* "please do it for me? Give it a chance? At some point, please."

It won't work. "Ok," I answered reluctantly, with withdrawal from the conversation. I honestly just needed it to be over.

"Wynn, do you think I'm stupid?... wait, don't answer that," *my snake tongue in the act of opening my mouth to agree to the question,* "I know you won't do it unless I force you to do it right now. So go."

He knows me well, but not well enough. If I make a promise I keep it. I stick to it. I rarely make a promise I can't keep, or I think I can't. That's why I can never, when I'm in the dumps, promise that I'm okay. I can say I'm okay, but not promise it. So if I say I'll go in and see her, I'll keep to my word. You may think I'm manipulative, sly, and smart, but I am much simpler than you may have hoped. I plan, I have to be in control of every situation, I'm manipulative, and I'm a bit paranoid; but I am true to my word. If I say I'll go, I'll go. But I can't promise that anything good will happen out of it.

"Fine," I didn't *want* to go, but I knew that, as stubborn as I am, Dew Itty is just as stubborn. It was a fight I wouldn't win, I had to give in.

Every muscle in my body and enacting, I pulled my body up. No one was around, so I didn't have to worry about someone seeing me. But it didn't matter. I knew what was happening, I was giving up. I was giving a chance to someone else to take my win, and I lose. But I'll still do it with grace and with my word intact. I'll keep to my promise. I looked down the hall and begin my journey. One foot in front of the other, I turn the corner and she was right down that last hallway. Trudging and inching closer and closer, her door was open like the gates of hell. The gates of hell with a nice, innocent angel within, but that did not make me feel any better.

Here goes nothing, "Hello?" Head peeped in, the most innocent and naive face glanced up to acknowledge me.
"Hi, come on in," *did she know I was going to come?*

The couches in her room rearranged similarly to the lounge, however, the place designated for the visitor was placed in the position where the door was not visible. The door is behind me. I felt at a loss of control. *Unease*, with critters crawling up my back and arms. Across from the seat for the prey, where I resided, the window glared at me judgingly. But the reflection only reflected back upon me and there was no door in sight. Just a quitter in the mirror.

"Sit down," Dr. Murial gestured me to take a seat in the hot seat, "Is there something I can do for you?"

Swallow a wad of spit and pride. "I think I need to talk."

"Ok, that's totally okay! I hope you know, before we start, this is a safe place. Everything you say is confidential, between just you and me. However, it would be a lie if I said that if something seemed really concerning and unsafe, I will have to report it. But I just want to be honest with you, like I would like you to be with me. So... what is it you would like to talk about today, Wynn?"

At least she was honest, she just revealed one of my concerns to be true; something I say can change everything for the worse if I come off as "unsafe" or "of concern". *Be cautious of the next few words, you always are, but this time it means so much more.*

"Can I be honest?"

"Of course! This is a safe place," *stop saying that.*

"This wasn't my idea... I don't think there is anything wrong with other people coming in here to talk to you, but this is new for me. I honestly feel really uncomfortable and I don't know why I'm here," I got straight to the point.

I'm not one to hold punches very often, I'm generally a straight shooter. I don't like to drag something out I think can be quickly and easily over. I didn't want her to think lowly of me, and I didn't want to show my weakness. She needed to know, I was in full control and I wasn't going to crack easily. If Dew Itty and Jean can't do it, there is no way this Dr. Murial can.

"I see... Why is that? Why do you think this other person told you you should consider coming in to see me?" *Challenged question.*

"I guess I'm stressed out, or at least appear to be."

"What are you stressed about?" *Like a digging gopher she kept going.*

"I have some things going on at home, unhappy personal things, and also I guess I could be stressed out with academics and school."

"Ok, if you don't mind me asking, what's going on at home? You don't have to answer unless you feel comfortable." *Nice try.*

"I don't feel comfortable sharing that."

"And that's okay," *I know.*

If anything, something important I've learned is that often the best way to manipulate someone to open up or break first, is the power of silence. As human beings, is a natural response to try to fill in all gaps of uncomfortable silence. I use this trick quite often actually, along with challenging questions; basically, Dr. Murial's method of trying to break me, I have used a million times before. I consider myself devilishly sly with a manipulative characteristic I inherited from the very people who hurt me. Actually, I am quite ashamed of this quality; I always fear I'll make someone feel the way my family makes me feel. I never want that, but it is a quality I possess and is hard for me to prevent. So instead, I use it for good; like Dr. Murial so clearly does. I use it to help people open up and to help people learn valuable lessons about their well-being, self worth, and self preservation. Dr. Murial was trying to do the same for me. I knew it, I was aware of it, and I would not allow her to win this conversation. I am a pro at this game, and there was no way I'd fall victim to my own tricks. I can't. I refuse.

But I did.

The moment of silence, as agonizingly uncomfortable as it was, wasn't what broke me. No, it was that look.

My gaze often darts back and forth when I'm in different environments in order for me to be able to catch all the details of my surroundings and for me to be in full control. I like to analyze a room right when I walk in. But this room had nothing in it that I could focus upon and analyze. It was a clean room, with a few plants and signs with encouraging messages; all I could analyze from that was that this woman, this doctor, was someone who highly believed in the "pinterest" esk solutions to mental health problems. The kind of solutions where you make everything look textbookly neat and aesthetically pleasing and fill your days with inspirational quotes. There was nothing personal in my eye view, so there was nothing of importance for me to analyze. All I saw was a room built for the poor hurt souls to come in and feel at ease and calm. All *I* felt was panic, because there was nothing I could figure out about my opponent through this room. My gaze was restricted and honed down to just allowing me to look at her. There are many things you can analyze and read about a person based on their person themselves. What their wearing, how they sit, how they respond to certain remarks, their facial features, facial expressions, and their whole demeanor are absolute giveaways for an investigator like myself. Usually, I'd bring it all down to a science and a consensus of the things I've learned about this character; but I was distracted.

I was too hyper-focused on figuring out what to say that all I could look at were her eyes. That direct eye contact broke me. Not the silence, the eye-contact. I broke. I lost, but I can't lose the whole war, just this battle.

> "I, in all honesty, don't want to tell you anything about my personal life or the events occurring around me. But, I do think it is important for me to talk to someone about my individual well being," I was ready to give her just that part and nothing more.

I put out my metaphorical hand and Dr. Murial went in to shake it. The deal was struck: I will email or contact her any time my own mind decides to backstab me; as long as she was aware of the fact I won in not telling her anything else, and won't be easily pried into to get that information out.

No, *I'm in control.*

Chapter 37

RECEDING IN THE UNSENT.

I sat here blank staring at a blank email to you. I know I'm supposed to reach out to you if I need anything, or if it feels like I'm getting worse. You are a professional in the field of the mind. I'm supposed to come in and talk to you, but I just can't bring myself to do so. You are just there at school, a counselor for the peers, but I can't do it. The things I want to actually say, I'm scared will scare you away; or worse, make you worry and actually help me.

How do I tell you I'm scared of myself?

> You ask me if I feel like at any point do I feel like my environment is not safe. I say no, but my first thought is the environment doesn't matter; because the worst things that cause me harm is myself. I'm scared about how far I've gone. I'm scared about how far my brain has gone. I don't want to come in to talk to you because I don't want to understand. I don't need my brain to hurt anyone else. I don't want to try anymore.
>
> I want to disappear.

But how do I tell you that without raising some red flags? Should I tell you?

Telling you will only help me, I know that. I continue to reassure myself that's why I should continue to do so; but I can't help but allow my brain to convince me that the more I share, the more havoc I'm causing for the people involved in my life. I feel like the weight of other people's lives rest on my shoulders, columns on a base. Any time wasted on fixing the base while the columns are still relying on me can only result in a higher chance of the collapse of one or all of the columns.

Is my life really more important than making sure that those columns don't fall? I can't seem to convince myself of that. I'd rather slowly crumble and let everyone solidly down on the ground than to try to fix something that has gone too far.

> "Everyone can be helped, it is impossible for there to be someone who can't be". I know you truly believe that, and I never said I can't be helped. I just can't be saved, and I'm starting to lose hope and feeling that help should be wasted on something that can't be saved.
>
> I'm done trying. I'm so tired of trying to find that silver lining I could never actually find. I'm a lost cause.
>
> I want to die.

*   *   *

But first this email

Chapter 38

THE FIRST TIME

Walking out of school, one foot after another, keys clenched between my fingers; I kept my head down and fast-walked towards my car. Hyper focused on my goal, I ignored the world like a computer doing the coded task for a direct solution. Emotionless, I don't feel like I'm thinking. My conscious is receding and backing away from my frontal lobe; simultaneously, joining my subconscious, hiding in the back of my skull. My car in view, I get to it and place my hand quickly on the doorknob and yank it open briskly. Feeling a small bit of pent up anger, unsure where to direct it; I centralize it into the feelings in my muscles. With every jerk, flex, and tug on my tendons; I feel my anger course through my veins. No words, not even a peep comes out of my mouth; this internal flame inflames every muscle in my body but can't manage to open my mouth. I get in my car and I drive. I drive like I have a fear of being late to no destination, but at the same time fighting to keep emotionless. Quick actions, I got out of the parking lot and headed home. Hitting the brakes quickly without deceleration, speeding up when the light turns green without acceleration.

Is it funny that she just realized that she was insignificant? Her body hit the floor, feeling every molecule in her body giving in and wanting to be pulled into the ground. Wanting the dirt to hug her like a coffin. She wished she could just wipe the pain off her life board like a clean slate, and she thought it was all her fault. She was negligible, no one noticed. Her body curled up into a ball, on the ground, in a room, with no windows or furniture; just her and her infinitesimal meaning.

If a tree falls in a forest and no one is around to hear it, does it make a sound? The definition of *sound* is there must be a recipient and someone who is around to hear the *sound*. But just because there is a sound, that doesn't make a difference because no one heard it. No one heard her body hit the pavement. No one heard her heart stop beating. No one knew the pain she had ridden the world of. Because she was insignificant, infinitesimal, negligible, and no matter whether she made a *sound*, it didn't make a difference.

In her head echoing in rhyme, her mind mocking in signs, lining up to cut her last string holding her up with every sigh:

I hate myself.
And I'm ashamed of hating who I am. I shouldn't hate
who I am because so many people don't.
People apparently care.
I don't feel it. I refuse to see it.
And of course that leads to...

(Cue THAT person)
"Your Brain is a jerk and you are just too
stubborn and insecure
to believe anyone cares,
but they do.
You just gotta let them in"

Yes, cause THAT makes me feel better.
I hate myself
For hating myself
And am ashamed of hating myself

For hating myself
And hating is just a cycle
A spiral
A swirl
That ends up
Twirling a girl
Into a
Whirl
Of
...

Chapter 39

NIGHTFALL'S TIME BENT

Time is running down to the chime.
Laying around trying to sleep,
The seconds tick to minutes.
Every *tick* agonizing
M whimpering heart with a haunting echo
in my empty skull.
Like hearing heels walking
click clunk click clunk,
Like a heartbeat effect in a game when tension is high
ba-Dum ba-Dum,
Like pulling the cord on the lawn mower to start
Cutting the old to give room to the new but
Failing to get it started
tick tick vrrr tick tick vrrr,
Like reloading a gun aimed at my heart because shooting one bullet
wound over and over again is satisfying
click click bang click click bang.

With every click of the clock,
And every tick of the sick,

I felt my heart sink
With every blink
I craved a shrink,
Fake sympathy for the weak.
I craved a link,
a split second for the meek
To descend down
And get a flicker
Of a meager
Shrug.

Don't stoop down
To get the lowly found
Forms of gratitude
When you deserve a world

Or maybe I'm lonely in my time alone
In my time to atone
In the shadow of the moon
I learn that's the time
Where sweets are taken like a lime
The positives in the day
Are turned astray.

It's too late
For me to have an amazing feat
Where I defeat
The leaves
Of my
Fall.

Chapter 40

JUST LIKE THAT

I can't go home. I just can't today.

It has become a bit of a therapy for me to drive around, and I had started to do it more often. It started out as a once-a-week thing and quickly escalated to 4-5 times a day. A quick relief to an addiction to escape. Just me and my yellow jeep.

Yellow. I originally decided upon the color because it is the happiest of colors, and G*d knows I need more of that. My happiness is an external locus, a feeling I could never feel internally. The happiest moments I've had weren't even mine. They were of the people I cared for and their joy, laughter, and childish behavior felt like a 'happy' I guess. It's not the same, but it is the best I can do and am familiar with. I take what I can get. Yellow was a wise choice I think, I do feel a level of serotonin from seeing my beautiful baby, Sunny Phi (yes, yes I named her). Also, did you know sunshine scientifically helps you produce more happy hormones? I didn't know that. But research shows it to be true! So I wanted a constant reminder that the world has things that can help me get some form or another of 'happy'.

Muscle memory took hold of my body and I started to feel more conscious of my body's weight. Breathing was strategic, but everything else felt involuntary. Driving aimlessly, like letting the wave take me to a pointless destination in the middle of the ocean. The minute I turned out of school, I felt my body go its usual route at the intersections and recalled every object, store, and person outside my car. Remembering everything. The elderly woman going on her daily walk in her very trendy activewear in an atrociously pertinent hot pink on the first block past the big intersection. The usual dog walker walking three miniature dogs across the street exactly on time at the intersection I turn left at first. I drive around this usual route every time, at this point, I can't manage to stop. It is so therapeutically consistent. Straight, turn, straight, turn, straight. Driving felt... *right*. At first, when I first started doing it, I felt a sense of relief and felt like I was finally able to run away from my life. I didn't have to think or feel anything. And soon, I couldn't. I couldn't feel anything or think anything. I soon began to dissociate while driving, losing track of time, worries, and safety.

Waking up in random parking lots of Jack-in-the-box's and coming-to at school on a weekend, I realized it has mutated from its purest form of coping to the monstrous haze of demonic possession leaving me to clean up the pieces and drive home. There was once I dissociated and came-to amidst driving recklessly quickly towards a brick wall because the feelings my unconscious felt overwhelmed the dissociated version of me. Not only had my conscious self been fed up so much that I began to dissociate, but also, my unconscious even wanted to rid the world of my baggage. *Skrrrrrtttt.* I swerved the car and slammed the break to a stop perfectly a few feet from the crash and the tombstone that lay ahead with my name claiming it. Without much more thought, a shrug, a twist, and a drop, I dropped the subject and immediately drove home without further thought or complete understanding of the recent occurrence. It just... it is what it is, and I have more than once overwhelmed myself in a deadly cycle of asking 'why' without any reasoning. I guess, I just realized that I'll never know and there is no point in fighting to find the answers.

I should go home.

Driving blindly, I drove in a haze and my whole body felt heavy in its driving. Strong turns and my stomach overturns, but recklessly

I continued to drive in this manner. Turning the corner, my house was dead ahead. *Turn. Turn. Just turn in.*

Nope.

Ok, loop around one more time and try again. It's okay, don't be too hard on yourself. *I should have been able to, it isn't that hard.* No, it's okay. Just breathe and try again. *God, I'm wasting time.* No, there is no time limit. Just try again. *Just turn in.*

Nope.

Loop.

Turn.

Nope.

Loop.

Turn.

Nope.

Loop.

Turn.

Finally, I turned into the little cul-de-sac that my house called home. Driving in, I opened the front gate and drove into my parking spot respectfully. *Get out and go inside.* That's nice, my body and brain are out of sync. I felt paralyzed in my car and could not manage to pull the strength out of my muscles to grab the door handle and open the door to my car. I was stuck. Stuck in my own car with my keys, my body, my brain, and my time. Stuck. I sat there for a solid 30 minutes just clenching my fists around the steering wheel unable to release. Every inch of my body inching towards just quickly backing out and going back on the road. Like a dog scared of a noise, I wanted to run in the opposite direction in a quick swift motion while barking a tantrum in rebellion to moving forward towards the danger. But the other side of me knew not to do that and knew that I can't always run away from my problems. *Face them*, not like a coward. *Just get out of the fucking car.* Nothing budged.

Ding.

My phone got a notification and immediately my body found a level of release to check the notification to pay attention to anything other than the entrapment the world afflicted upon me. It was a text from Jean Louise. I clicked the notification on the dashboard of my car and Siri promptly stated, "Hey! I just wanted to say I love you. Also, by chance do you want to come over? I can't concentrate and I kind of want to study with someone. If you can't we can facetime? *Smiley face with hearts.*"

Jean Louise has a tendency to overly express a sense of love, and I usually brush it off. She knows I by no means am doing so because I don't care about her back, I do. I just am poor with emotions of affection because I don't understand the proper response. I have never understood it and don't assume that anyone could care that way. But besides the point... maybe I can just come over there. It might be easier than trying to defeat this mental block. Also, technically, I'm not running away like a coward; I'm running away to help someone else like a hero, not a coward running away from my own trouble. *Yes. I'll come over.*

I've been doing that every time now, even when Jean Louise doesn't need anything. I just... come over. It has come to the point that now Jean and Bailey think of me as the friend who is impulsive and simply just comes over whenever I'm bored and am down to do things impromptu. It definitely isn't because I'm running away from my issues, *of course not.* I tell Jean more than I tell Bailey because emotionally, Bailey and I don't share much. But that is what is beneficial to me in our relationship. Jean and I's relationship work from a sense of vulnerability, more from her than me but still. So at some point, I ended up telling Jean about my mental block to my own house, and her mother was told as well. Both she and her mother welcomed me to come over if I ever need to. So I did.

Mrs. Mariane Louise, Jean's mother, served like another mother for me and I trust her like I would with my 'own' mother... but I actually talk to her. My mother and I don't have much of a talking relationship because I never see her and I can't explain anything to her. She genuinely believes I am just a moody teen who isn't chronically suffering in my own reveling self-guilt. I don't talk to her. I am worried about making her worried and going through the things I've been through, I have always been alone. I can't trust anyone. I can't be fully honest; I guess, a part of me knows, if I talk to my mother, I can't help but be truthful. Looking into her eyes, I'll give in and tell her. *I can't tell her. I can't. If I tell her, it'll hurt her so much and she will blame herself. She will feel responsible for something she shouldn't feel responsible for. I shouldn't feel responsible but I do, and I don't want her to feel that way. I have to avoid her, or I will break and tell her the truth. More than anything, I want to be able to go home and feel like I can be safe and truthful, leaving the pain and deceitful world outside. More than anything, I want to be able to just be vulnerable and ask for my mother's help.* But I don't talk to her because I *never* see her, that is *why. Not because I can't tell her. That is the only reason.*

One day my mother texted me when I informed her I was at the Louise home and it was a text that riddled me with guilt in ways that I don't think anyone will ever understand:

"You can't always go to Jean's house. I am your mother, come home to me. You can't run away from your problems and create a new reality for yourself. I am your family, come home. Stop running away from home and going to someone else's house to make a new family. I am your mother, Mrs. Louise is not. Come home now." *Just like that. It's easy.*

Chapter 41

DOMINOES AND SCALES

Let's dissect that:

Everyday since the day I was born, I have always questioned my choices in everything and every word. I've always believed my words have power, and every word has to be worth the breath that lets it out. Every action has an infinite amount of possibles as a result, but there are only a few outcomes that are most likely to occur depending on who is involved. Then, it's time to see what is the outcome you want, despite the pros and cons that every single one holds. Which one has the most pros for those involved? Is it worth it? What can I do to ensure the outcome be that? Is it worth it? Who gets hurt?

I was quiet as a kid, and I didn't waste my words like I had a limited amount. I listened, I obeyed, and I contained. I didn't let any go, and with that I soon learned the value of every single word and action. Life worked like dominoes. Breathe on the first word just wrong, and it sets off a chain of events to come. I can argue this point as much as I want just by stating it to be true, but you probably won't believe me. Let me prove it.

Hanging on every word, the most extreme example:

Suicide.

You read that, what was your initial thought? If I'm wrong, oh well; but I'm going to guess: when you read that you felt a breath leave your body, like the energy in your body lowered a bit to something more somber; ready to know where the word will go, but still leaving you cautiously stepping from fear of what you are about to read. Overall, a slight sense of sympathy and feeling bad for what you are about to read even before reading what I have to say. Subconsciously without realizing it, you've decided there is a victim to be sorry for. That was *one* word. But no, that wasn't my whole proven point.

I have had several friends who have been suicidal before, and everytime that they felt that way they would call me or text me. They wouldn't tell me directly that they were feeling that way, but I could feel it. I could sense the pain in their words in their texts, every last bit of lingering energy in each character, and every tear shed with every heartfelt random act of admiration as to say goodbye. Sometimes it's an apology apologizing for everything they never did, apologizing for every negative emotion or feeling they never inflicted upon you, and/or apologizing for just being. Sometimes it's a heartfelt act of admiration. Telling you they love you, telling you they treasure you more than anything, and/or telling you how much they appreciate the fact you *had* crossed their path. Their wording and knowing them for who they are, I knew. Their words were screaming for them without them needing to make a peep. Talking them through it, my words mattered too. I knew how to talk to them individually with enough sense of who they are, what they would listen to in the state of mind they were in, and keeping cautious of what would send them over the edge. I have prevented my friends from committing suicide more than once and for more than one friend. My actions and words mattered, but there was one time I almost lost someone because I had forgotten to consider every single one of my words and every single one of my actions towards seeing them for *them*.

> *"Hey, random thought: I can't believe I'm so lucky to know you. You are great, you have been there for everyone and you are the strongest person I know. You have a strength uncomparable to anyone else, but you*

are tired. I know. And I feel bad for being that burden for you, I am sorry for everything negative I've ever done to you. I'm sorry for hurting you. I'm sorry for being a horrible friend. I'm sorry for not appreciating you for everything you are, but instead, using you till you feel burnt out. It's like I'm using you. I'm sorry. You really have changed my life so much, and I couldn't imagine how my life would be like without you. Really. I love you, and I'm sorry for not being good enough. You should take a break from me, you need it. You don't need me to drag you down anymore."

Reading through their text, I analyzed every word and phrase carelessly disregarding who they were and viewed it mechanically like any other suicidal situation I had stumbled upon before.

This text was chalk-full of random sincere apologies for things out of their control and contained several acts of random admiration towards me, and so my thoughts went directly to the fact that my friend was probably fairly suicidal at the moment.

What did I do? Well I went through a mechanical and logical process of texting them back and doing the minimalistic thing to make sure they survived, neglecting them personally. *Are you safe right now? What is wrong? You're not a burden to me. I love you too. You shouldn't be sorry if you didn't do anything wrong, and you didn't. There are a million things out of your control, and that is okay.*

And I left it.

At that.

Reaching over to a knife, they slit their wrists while I was texting them. No response, like a dead ECG and radio silence. My heart started to ache and unsettled. My stomach churned, and my brain knotted. I got worried sick, like my guts would just spill out. I got up and called to them. *No answer.* I promptly got up and tried to sprint to the door, I got to go see them. I had to make sure they were safe, but I slipped. Unknowingly, I had been sobbing and my tears flooded the floor mixing in with the reds and diluted pinks. Dripping down my cheeks and down my hands, my blood, sweat, and tears mixed. My foot dipped into the blood already on the floor and I ended up laying on the ground helpless, and unable to stand. *Breathe in. Breathe out.* All I could think was, I have to help them. They need me. *GET UP!* Why do I feel so helpless? How could I slip up on my words and limbs when they are so important to me?

I layed there for some time. Numb but feeling at the same time. My body and arm fell limp, but my heart and mind throbbed for them. I layed in my pitiful uselessness. *I can't even get up, how can I be of any importance in helping anyone?*

My arm had already begun to clot and my blood was no longer dripping all over, and I managed to stop my tears from overflowing. I couldn't save myself. I could save every single other person who has come to me with their suicidal thoughts, but the one person I have never treated like a human was the one person I needed help saving: myself. I never considered myself as someone who needed to be considered, and I ended up self harming. Every cut made in my arm, each relieving numbness with a physical feeling. Any cut not deep enough to feel, I would reinflict it. Over and over. Until it was an addiction. Because I never considered another solution. My words weren't the solution. But it was all because every word matters. And every person matters.

I'm sorry to my past self. I didn't mean to hurt you.

Chapter 42

BODILY RELATIONSHIP

It's textbook, really. As a teen, it is normal to develop a fascination with perfecting our self image and try to conform our bodies to fit the societal liking. This isn't news. Every teen has heard about how we should embrace our bodies no matter the size, weight, or what social media or magazine girls in bikinis try to force us to look like. I think our self images of independent strong women and men breaking toxic sex norms is at its peak, and will continue to escalate! ... *that's what my logical data driven mind would say, but this doesn't deprive the struggle from still occurring.*

When I was born, I was underweight. I had trouble eating and I was a child of great troubles for my parents. I would never swallow and I didn't chew. At some point I was way under weight in comparison to other kids my age. My parents began to give me this concoction that was supposed to help me gain weight to become normal. It was called Ensure. I continue to drink it and I did so because I wanted to make my parents a little bit happier because of the burden that I caused them. It was my fault I think. My parents say it was genetic but I think it was my fault. If I only figured out how to eat earlier. I continue to drink it and gained a lot of weight. I accidentally continued to drink it past the point where I was normal weight and gained a lot of 'baby fat'. Or at least that's what I called it since I was still a little.

From a young age, I never cared for my looks. I wasn't confident by any means; I just didn't care what anybody said about me except for a select amount of people. I cared about what my mother said about me. I cared about what my sister said about me. And I cared about what my dad said about me. The rest of the world didn't deserve a chance to bring me down; but they did. A common cultural thing that every relative of mine went through when we were little was that our parents would dress us up in a majority of unisex clothing, full coverage clothing, and cut our hair into bowl cuts. I distinctly remember my parents constantly wanting me to match with my sister in thick light yellow sweat sets and they sent us to school like two baby Dora's in the unforgiving heat. I was too young to question it; my sister wasn't. Soon in lower school, my sister ended up finding her own style and leaving me behind in the baggy clothing. She complained constantly about how it was ugly, it was uncomfortable, and how she hated being so similar to me. Without outwardly exclaiming so, I honestly felt really comfortable in it. The baggy clothing made me feel secure in my body without having to worry too much about trying to compete with anyone else; because they didn't know, they didn't see my body. I didn't care what anybody else said but as my sister began to complain about the clothing, I felt subconsciously that she was complaining about me. She didn't want to be like me. Why would she? I wanted to be like her. But I couldn't compete because we were built very differently. Our bodies were of different forms, shapes, and weight. I couldn't do anything about it as she left me in the dust.

"Daddy?" I walked into the bathroom. Water was pouring down the drain and the heat began to caress my body. I was young, I don't member how old. I walked into the bathroom without fear and without regret. I walked in with a mission. "Daddy?" My small voice remarked as I looked upward towards the sky and saw his face. He looked at me from inside the shower, past the glass, and asked me what I was doing there. I laid my face against the glass door and placed my hand on the glass knowing I couldn't reach in and be the version of myself I longed for. It wasn't a glass ceiling I could break through, it was a glass barrier guarded by the only people I listened to. "Yes, Thành?" "I want that," I answered as I indicated my longing to have a dick. *I want to be a boy. I hate my body because it constricts me from being my full potential to make you proud. If I was just a boy, you would be proud. You would love me. You would accept me. I wouldn't feel so wrong. I wouldn't feel... like a mistake.*

He laughed at me. Culturally and also generationally, my parents didn't even allow the thought I was transgender to cross their minds. It was just *funny* and a *joke*. I moved on and grew up in my body. My female body.

I continued to dress this way all through the first half of middle school. My sister did not. She was dressing trendy and everybody loved her style. Her appearance mattered because... again... it's textbook. According to the psychology of attraction, one of the main motivators of attraction is physical attraction. Something I lacked. I had no style, no confidence, no social skill, and no comfortability in my own being. I didn't hate my body... I just didn't like it. It made me squirm.

Puberty. Puberty hit me at around 7th grade but inconsistently. My period was and still is inconsistent to rare, and I didn't mind it. I never understood girls who like to talk about their periods. Like you're speaking to each other about blood leaving your body, and somehow that makes you more womanly? How does bleeding and hurting and pain mean you're a woman? If my period is so inconsistent does that mean I'm less of one? Do I mind it? I just think the idea of speaking to other females about my genitalia is uncomfortable. I'd rather leave that to the experts. My body begin to develop in other areas as well. It's a given that my breasts will develop, my voice, and a larger sense of sexuality. My voice, unlike other people, did not get more feminine. Well my other friends that are females were getting a lot more girly and womanly and alluring to the heterosexual horny teen male perspective, I became more independent. After puberty my body became more feminine and developed curves that I couldn't accept. My breasts grew and I covered them. Well other girls were flaunting them for more popularity and likes on Instagram, I hid them from myself. I didn't care what other people saw, I didn't want to see it. From drinking Ensure so much as a child, when I reached puberty, I discovered a new side of myself. A stronger and more buff looking self. I felt more masculine. A little more close to comfortable. In retrospect, though I gained more of a breast, I also gained more perspective and confidence in what I wanted to see in my own body instead of being as ashamed as I was prior.

High school. *Sigh*. I recently came out as genderfluid and I have had more issues with my body in high school that I have ever had prior. If you don't know, gender fluid means that there are moments where I feel and identify with being more masculine and male and other times I feel/identify with being more feminine and slimmer. Because of that I end up having a lot of problems. My body can't just shape shift along with Genderfluidity. So many times I've looked at my body and gotten so angry with myself because I don't look as masculine as I'd like to. I picked up working out and doing weights in order to improve my body into something more masculine. But physically my body can't look exactly like the one of a mail. I simply wasn't born with the genetics of a biological male body. I don't want to be a male but sometimes I identify as one. I also can't count the number of times I have completely forgotten that I am not in a male body. I relate strongly with my guy friends physically, emotionally, and mentally. The number of times I forget that I don't have a dick is a phenomenal number. But I remember. I always come back to it. This is all because I also sometimes identify with my female body. Moments where I feel girly, wanna wear a dress, want to put on makeup, take pictures, dance around in heels, and just giggle with my friends that are girls are moments that I feel like I'm on cloud nine. I'm a girl. Those are moments where I forget that I have ever had problems with my body. Because I have been so gracefully granted a body that has curves, makes me feel sensual in my own skin, it makes me feel happy. But on the other hand I also have moments where I think that my body is way too fat. I gain too much weight. I looked too masculine now. I wish I was slimmer in a bikini. I wish I looked curvier. I wish I looked like her. I wish I looked like... anyone else. I have my moments where I am up in moments where I'm down. But in all honesty after coming out, I love my body. I'm confident in who I am and confident in my identity. And I'm grateful to have found out. I'm not transgender, because if I had identified myself as transgender prior, I wouldn't have appreciated how much I like being a female. But I also love being a male.

Though it seems as if my journey with my physical body is completely separate from my mental health, it's actually all connected. Culturally, when you look at any famous or beloved Asian female or male, I am not that. Their skin is pure as Snow, their hair is a dark and silky smooth black, and they are super skinny. My skin easily tans, and I can't do anything about it. My mother has tried. She gave me the soap when I was younger to use to make my skin lighter and make me look a lot daintier; but I didn't use it. I used it for a short period of time because I wanted to be seen as beautiful from my mother. I care what she says and what she thinks. But after a certain point I stop doing it because I knew that if I started to do it and I wanted to maintain it I would have to do it for the rest of my life. That is because genetically I can't change who I am. No soap can change who I am. My hair is not dark and silky smooth black. I was born with hair that is easily changed. Anytime I stayed out in the sun for too long it became lighter. When I was younger my hair was basically brown with hints of light brown at the top of my head but it was still dark. But I still didn't reach that maximum goal of black. And I wasn't skinny. Not anymore anyway. The only thing that I could control was my weight.

This is also connected to my mental health. Because I was born with depression and my depression affects my physical health extremely easily, it wasn't too big of a jump for me to start realizing that I developed an eating disorder. The first thing to go physically was my sleep. When my depression got really bad, I couldn't sleep three days in a row every week. I thought it was just insomnia, I thought it was normal. It took a toll on me. At times it was even painful. My whole body felt like it was in a paralysis where I just could not get out of bed some days but I just laid there with my eyes wide open. I had no control. My sleep schedule went out the window and soon my hygiene. I couldn't maintain my hygiene because I was so tired, so drained, and it just didn't cross my mind that there were things that I needed to do to take care of myself. And along with that, eating. I stopped eating. I stopped eating for several reasons, and they're not reasons that I am proud of. Firstly, I couldn't eat. I didn't feel hungry, I didn't feel motivated, and I forgot that that was an essential part of being alive. When you feel like your brain is trying to kill you and quench you off of this planet earth, eating just doesn't pop up as a top priority anymore. I physically couldn't get myself to eat. I looked at food and wanted to throw up. I thought about food and I started to get more depressed. I knew that I couldn't eat and I wanted to. Secondly, I associated eating with bad things. After my sexual assault, I didn't want to eat anymore. My body didn't feel like the way that I did before. I didn't want to take anything anymore. My dad would constantly ask me if I wanted to eat, and I couldn't. I associated eating with him. I associated living with my depression. And I associated my body with the disrespect that it went through. I lost any confidence I had in my own body for being something I could love. I lost it all. And I stopped caring about it. I stopped respecting it. I was harming it. Physically now. Not feeding it, not giving it nutrients, not letting it rest, and also cutting it. Cutting it slowly, piece by piece. On a level, I disassociated from it, it wasn't me. I didn't care for it.

Time has passed since my sexual assault. And I've become a lot more comfortable again with my body. I don't necessarily treat it the same way I did before, but at least now I respect it. I respect that my body sometimes will react and that my mental will help my physical. I give myself room to react. I don't judge myself for doing so. And I feed myself with food and respect and comfort because if no one else has ever given that to me and Will ever give that to me, I will. My mental and physical are related and they will always be there for each other. I will always be there for me.

Chapter 43

IT'S ONLY REAL IF YOU SEE IT

Generational difference and cultural difference has enough effect on the outlook on mental health disorders. It is hard for my parents and my family members to understand. But I've come to understand that that doesn't matter, as long as they respect it; it is enough.

It is hard for my parents to understand or believe in my depression. My mom didn't believe or understand until she saw me in the hospital. She didn't understand until I was physically in danger from myself. Every mark on my arm terrified her. It terrified her even more she had never noticed it before. And the thing that terrified me the most was that she didn't understand how to fix it. She can't. It's not that simple, no matter how much we both wish it was.

Fuzzy. My world turned fuzzy. All my senses lost their flare for their skills, and I couldn't see, hear, feel, taste, or smell anything properly. I didn't feel like I was in my body. I couldn't think straight, the only thing I knew for sure was I wanted to feel. Quit this nonsense of numbness. Just stop it. Quit it. Stop.

My body began to move on it's own. Arms grabbing around the stomach and clawing. Squeezing and trying to rip off the piece of flesh to feed to the monster. It needed meat. It needed food. I had to feed it. My hands were steady as rocks as it continued to get some kind of feeling out of my body. Anything. Feel anything. Just feel.

I was up. My legs walked me to the destination that my body knew where to go. Walking aimlessly without the knowledge of my mind. *Where was I going?*

Clawing the X-acto knife out of it's box, my hands were steady and ready. Willing to do everything and anything it took to make it out of this fog, away from the monster. Eyes deadset on my skin, next thing I knew. Blade to flesh, I cut. It was like unlocking a new level. I was released. A level of relief I finally felt and my body felt everything again. And the fear began to set in.

What did I just do? I grew up knowing it was wrong. How could I? Why? Don't do that ever again. Oh My God. Oh My God. What did I just do? I dropped the knife and ran to the bathroom and looked in the mirror. Reasoning through with myself about what just happened. The pros and cons were apparent, and the cons overruled the cons. But I remembered that feeling. That instant relief. That instant sense of feeling. It was like an instant high. I was shocked I could feel for once. I could feel. I've never felt like that before.

Everytime after that, I told myself I would never do it again. But *Lies. All lies.* Time after time, I continued to cut myself. Mark after mark. Instantaneous feeling leading to quick and long-lasting regret. Regret while watching my arm cut open, and regret even after it scars over. Scars. Regret and shame. I can't explain the shame that comes from these scars. Scars mark our battle scars and mark our brilliant pride from our fights, but this isn't a battle scar. It's a self-inflicted drug. A drug I feel so shameful of.

Recently, my mom gave me the opportunity to go see a plastic surgeon with the possibility of ridding myself of my scars. But I said no. I don't self-harm anymore, but I needed the scars. The scars humbled me. Everytime my mom sees them, she cries. Her heart hurts from the pain that she couldn't shield me from. She is my mother. She will always not be able to blame herself for not being able to protect me from depression, or pain. She will always think its partially her fault. And she doesn't want me to be marked for the rest of my life by something that I used to feel ashamed for. But no longer. I am accepting of them now. On occasion, I feel self-conscious and hide them under long sleeves and jackets; but generally, I just remind myself it is a marker. Like a height marker we used to keep to tally how tall we were getting through time, this marker marked my growth. I've grown.

Chapter 44

50:50

Recently, it's felt like everything is 50:50.
50 : 50
Split the deal.
I'll take half, yours' left.
Enough to buy a meal,
But not the chef.

50 : 50
It's okay what you feel
Let's be real:
This is good, it's a steal
But it's bad in the real.

50 : 50
It makes a hundred
Without men dead.
We can split the deal
I'll take half, you'll feel
That this is the way to heal.

50 : 50
It's a fifty:fifty situation
A happy place for taking,
But a disaster in the making.

50 : 50
Feeling fifty:fifty about every
Situation, merry
But scary.

50 : 50
I'm 50% certain I'm dead alive
But 50% certain I'm living dead.

Heads or tails,
We'll split the deal
I'll take half,
What's left is sealed.

Chapter 45

A STAY AT HOSPITAL HOTEL

I woke up paralyzed.
Heavily dragged down like a tree taking root into the ground stretching towards the earth's core to give it a hug. Dragged into the warm, cozy feathers of the bed that coddled me like a nest.

You're being dramatic. Just get up.

But I can't. My logical mind is screaming to move. My computer mind is pulling the metaphorical strings to tug me out of bed. Playing tricks and jumping jump ropes trying to hoax the weight on my emotional brain to relent reigns of my physical body. No amount of clever wordplay was getting me to get out of this jumble.

Fine. Don't move then, you pathetic, over dramatic teen. You'll miss school again. You are so useless, just die already and give a real reason to not go to school.

Ah, classic argumentative, computational, logical brain. Switching sides to not look like a loser, but ultimately feeding into the depression's ail. *If you can't beat them, join them, and do it like a boss.*

I've done this before. Some mornings (who am I kidding)... most mornings, I struggle to get out of bed and find a solid reason to. I simply feel like a dead weight. As a result, my school attendance is flawed, *obviously.* My mother tries to save me from getting unexcused absences, and comes up with excuses to get me excused. But today was different. It was like the council in my mind all shook hands in agreement and came to the conclusion that I should reach out to the school counselor this time. She always said that I should email her if I had concerns or I needed to. I felt it about time I dealt with my issue of feeling this way. I want to know how to fix it. I want to be back to normal again… or at least a little bit, and go back to school. *I'll be responsible and honest this time. I'll be a good person and not lie… this time.*

I emailed her. And I didn't get a response. I fell back asleep.

Pop! My eyes finally opened again and the weight had not left, it lingered but it had lessened. I couldn't get myself to sit up and get out of bed, so I rolled out. I rolled out onto the ground and layed on the ground, embracing the impact. Hugging the floor, I stretched my hand out to grab my phone that was lying on there. I must have kicked it off the bed somehow. Or something. I don't know. On my stomach, I tapped the little screen. It's 12 in the afternoon now. My mom texted me a couple hours prior.

"Come upstairs. We need to talk."

That seems sketchy. Get up. Get up and go upstairs to talk to your mother. After a few more minutes of stretching on the ground, I pulled myself up. *Drag your ass upstairs.*

"Honey, what's wrong?" *Everything. That's a stupid question.*
"What do you mean?"
"I got a call from Dr. Murial from school. I didn't answer but then she texted me. She said you can't go to school until I take you to the hospital and get you diagnosed. She said you were suicidal and we needed to go today. If I don't take you, you are not permitted to go to school, not until we go and get this form filled out."

I see what Dr. Murial is alluding to. She doesn't have to soften the blow. She's worried that I will hurt someone or hurt myself if I go to school. I am a harm to those around me, because my spiral is like a tornado no one was ready for. I am not allowed to go back to school till I fill out this stupid form by a hospital diagnosis because I am meant to be in the emergency room. I am an *emergency…* no, a *hazard*. Just say it. Don't lie to me, and don't lie to my mother.

"okay." *There wasn't much choice, was there? Just so we are clear: I'm doing this so that Dr. Murial does not think I am going to harm anyone and I am doing this so my mom doesn't get stressed about how I'm physically not allowed to be on campus.*

"We need to go at like 7 tonight because I have to go to work right now."

"okay."

I simply layed in bed for the rest of the day anticipating my hospital trip, anxiously furiated at how Dr. Murial went behind my back and did this to me and anxiously unwilling to find out what's wrong with me. I don't want to be diagnosed. I… I'm scared.

I got sent to the emergency room waiting area. It was all a blur.

"Do you have a plan?"

"I've had a plan before."

"Have you been suicidal today?"

"Yes."

"How often do you have these thoughts?"

"I don't know, I don't keep track."

"Okay, I am going to say you go to the emergency room right now and wait because I can not allow you to go home now, because you are not safe to do so." *I get it. Now you know, I am now your responsibility. I can't die on your watch.*

I waited and moved around for about an hour from room to room, and finally they got me a room to reside in. There was a woman there to proctor me, because I am not allowed to be left alone at any point in time. *I hate it. I like privacy, but I respect it.*

176

"Hello! Has no one come by to get you into a gown yet? You kind
of have to in order to avoid you possibly trying to injure
yourself with zippers, items of clothing, and etc. Sorry. I
hope that is okay."

"Hello. Not yet, but okay. That's okay." *I don't have a choice but
thank you for making me feel like I do.*

"Oh, here, let me get you one!" the nurse scurried to get me
garments and came back and gave me a hospital gown,
"Let's go get you changed!"

"Okay." I followed her to the nearby bathroom and she walked
in with me.

Blink. Blink.

"Oh, I'm sorry. I have to stay inside here with you because I can't
leave you alone. If it makes you uncomfortable, I can turn
around."

Nod. I feel so uncomfortable being naked. I always feel
uncomfortable being naked. Something about it takes
me back to a feeling of being gross, nasty, and paranoid.
I don't have a choice though, I can't say no. I grabbed
the garments and stripped down to my skin. *God I wish
I could at least just wear a bra and underwear. I'd feel
better if I could.*

"I'm done, do you mind tying the back for me please?"

"Of course!" the nurse turned around promptly and tied the back
of the gown and essentially saw my whole bare skin hide.
Like a boar, I felt skinned down to my toes, "Okay! Let's
head back. I will take your clothes, I need to stick it in a
bag for sanitary reasons and so you can't reach it to get
possible usages of your clothes for injury. Oh. Also, I need
to take your phone, or you can give it to your mom." *I
gave it to my mom.*

I layed in the bed and pulled the covers over myself entirely, trying
to hold my breasts and limbs tightly to my body. I was struggling to

grapple with any sense of control that I felt I had lost when I lost my covering. I didn't say anything though. I just curled into a ball.

> "There is going to be a doctor who is going to come in to check your health, blood, pee, etc. in a bit. I am going to lock your stuff in this cabinet and then I have to go help someone else."

Nod.

My mom was in the room with me for half an hour or so as we waited. I turned on the tv and I continued to hug my breast tightly. My mom suddenly asked me if I was okay. *Nod.*

> "I told your dad that you are in the hospital because I thought I should tell him. He's so weird. He didn't respond to it, he just asked me about the altar at home for Ba (my grandma who has passed away)." *I didn't expect anything at all, so I wasn't surprised. I guess he still surprises her. Wow.*

> "Hello!" a female doctor entered the room alongside another nurse.

> "Hello."

> "Any complications so far?" the doctor asked the nurse watching over me this whole time and received a little laugh. *I suppose that was supposed to be funny, but it honestly just made me realize they deal with this all the time. I was just another teenager who's dramatic about pulling through on dying.*

> "Hello!" she turned to me, "So I am going to have to draw some blood for testing. I'm mostly just testing for health. But first…"

> *She touched me.* My breath escaped my lungs and stayed constant like a rock for a second. I can't breathe. Why did you just touch me?

> "I need to check your body for scars and any marks to make sure that you don't leave with any new marks and also to help

178

access how much self-harm you have done." *Panic. My breathe began to shorten and my lungs struggled to sound normal.*

Without asking like I had a choice, this doctor got to the point and just went for it. She untied the back of my gown and checked my back, my stomach, my arms, my legs and as many places as possible. I feel claustrophobic in her hands. I simply sat there powerless as she spoke out loud to the nurse about every mark, every scar, and every mark of self-harm on my body. ALL. OUT. LOUD.

"Okay. Wow that's a lot." the doctor said to the nurse as she looked at the notes sheet, "Okay, now we need to draw your blood."

I'm not scared of needles. Since I was little, I've never been scared of needles. I've also had so many experiences with needles for vaccines and also giving shots.

*   *   *

Ring. Ring. I picked up the phone.
"Hello?"
"Thành? I'm driving your mom home right now from the hospital. She had surgery and I need you to get your dad to help me get her to her room."
Without warning, I found out my mom had surgery that day. Apparently she was bleeding a lot and she had to have these two blood sacks attached to her body. She couldn't walk and she called our family friend to pick her up from the hospital. Instead of calling me, my dad, or my sister; she called our family friend. I get it. I know how suffocating our family can be, so I didn't blame her. I just was worried about her condition. I really hope to never have to see her in an instance where she looks like she was dying, but I might have to. Seeing my mother with two blood bags swing from her body, it

179

was my worst nightmare. I just wanted to help her get better and feel painless.

I ran to get my dad because I knew I would need his help. His response was not like mine. He was angry. He was frustrated. He'd rant about how this felt like déjà vu to my mom's cancer. She kept him in the dark again. He felt upset that he wasn't the first person she told. I'm not the person to tell him this, but honestly, he should be more concerned about her health than who she goes to first. But it isn't my place to tell him what to feel or not to feel. We waited anxiously. Or more like, I waited and he ranted. My sister was nowhere to be found. She was out with her friends.

Lights flashed through the glass front door, and that was our queue that our family friend's car had arrived. I ran out the front door to my mother. She couldn't get out of the car on her own, and she was in a lot of pain. My dad ran inside to grab a rolling chair, and I helped her sit in it. But he didn't think ahead. My mother's room is upstairs, so we couldn't roll her up. My dad attempted to try to do so similarly to how people do with little babies in strollers. But I saw my mom wince and I quickly came to her rescue, neglecting my dad's existence. I helped my mom stand up and we gave each other a look of agreement and I helped her walk up the stairs slowly. Step by step. And it was mostly me going on a step higher and lifting her up to relieve her of weight to walk up. When we finally made it upstairs, my dad started complaining. I ignored him and put my mom down in the desk chair she had in her room softly. After making sure she was okay sitting, I turned to my dad and said, "we need to tilt the bed a bit to allow her blood to flow so it is better". He agreed and we found two pieces of long planks of wood. I lifted the bed on one side as he put the planks under to create a tilt. After doing so, I walked over to my mom and lifted her up. I didn't let my dad touch her. I knew she didn't want him to. And I slowly lifted her weight and walked her slowly to the bed and laid her down.

Our family friend handed me a little white binder and told me the doctor told her to do and fill out the things in the binder to monitor her status. She whispered to me, "I don't trust your dad to do it and I don't trust your sister either. Read it." *Nod.*

My dad went downstairs and began to try to cook food for my mom. He was cooking some hot porridge soup for her. Our family friend left and went home.

Finally, I was alone with my mom. Kissing her on the forehead, I asked if she was okay. She smiled and said she was a bit uncomfortable but that was a given with the bloody sacks attached to her body. I nodded and sat on the ground next to her bed. "I'll stay here," and she nodded. I opened up the binder and began to read.

I had to help my mom empty her blood sacks and measure how much it was throughout time, and watch as the amount lessens. I would have to help my mom go to the bathroom because she couldn't get up on her own. I also had to help my mom get food and write down what she ate on a schedule. I had school though, so I adjusted the schedule to my school schedule so I would make sure I could be home to monitor her and help her. Finally, I had to give my mom a shot every 12 hours. Since I had school, I would get up at 4 in the morning to give my mom a shot and then when I got home from school give her another shot. Every time I would ask her, "Are you ready?" *Nod.* "Okay, here it goes." I would grab the vial of medicine and grab the needle. Insert it slowly and measure out the perfect amount. It was a shot that I had to keep steady as I pressed it in and I tried my best to not be too hasty to pull it out. I had to do a thorough job. I had to do this right. I continued to do so for about a week as my mom began to recover. No one else in my family offered to do any of it, I took the reins and was there for her.

*　　　*　　　*

"Do you need a countdown?"

"No." The nurse nodded and inserted the needle into my arm. No blood came out.

"What? Your vein was right there. I'm sorry. I'm so sorry. I think

181

your vein moved," she took the needle out and shook my arm a bit and tried again. No blood.

"Do you want to try on my other arm instead?"

"Sure. Let's try that," I pointed at the prominent place to stick the needle in and she did so accordingly and blood began to draw. She drew a little blood and then left. The doctor looked at me and then said, "I need you to pee in a cup."

God, this is my worst nightmare. I don't drink enough water to begin with and my bladder endures like a squirrel clinging to a tree branch upside down for its life. I let out a little laugh and honestly responded, "That might take a little while."

She laughed and said, "That's okay. Just do it. I will get you some water," she gestured to the nurse watching over me to type in an order for a water bottle.

Then the doctor and that one nurse left again. I was alone in the room naked under a hospital gown hugging my body, with my mom and the nurse watching over me. I sat in the room for a couple hours doing nothing other than drinking a lot of water. The nurse told me that I would have to wait a while until someone could come and give me a diagnosis and someone was free to see me. So I waited. Drinking water bottle after water bottle, waiting to pee and waiting to leave.

I was there for *three* more hours.

"Hello? Wynn?" a kind, almost comfortable, voice spoke through the doorway.

"Hello."

"Hi, Wynn! I'm so sorry for making you wait. There are just so many people and I'm sorry that no one has put you up higher in priority."

"It's okay, I understand," I smiled.

"So, this is how this is going to work. I am going to talk to your mother first alone in another room. And then I am going to come in here to talk to you without anyone else in the room with us. Whatever we talk about will be confidential, unless it is of extreme concern for your safety or others safety. I want to be completely honest with you, and I hope you are comfortable enough to be a little open with me," I nodded and felt comfortable with her.

"Okay! So, momma, let's go outside and talk."

I waited in the room with the nurse watching me alone for about 30 minutes. It felt longer. It didn't feel like thirty minutes, it felt like a grueling hour of anxiety. *I have been in here for way too long.*

"Hello?"

"Hello."

"Hi, Thành Phi! So now, we are going to talk," immediately the nurse took the hint and left. *Wow. The power this woman holds.*

"So, basically I am here to help you figure out what are the next steps and what we can do to help you by figuring out the issue. Okay?"

"Okay."

"So, I know starting out, this is a little awkward to just start talking, so I am going to ask you some questions. Okay?"

"Okay."

"So, what brought you in today? Do you know why you are in the emergency room?"

"My school counselor was concerned that I was suicidal and concerned that I would injure myself, and I am here because she said I wouldn't be able to go back to school unless I got a diagnosis of whatever was wrong with me."

"I see. Are you suicidal? Do you feel safe at home?"

"I have my moments. I at times get overwhelmed by a blur of feeling and the only comprehensible thought is the urge to cut the string of my life then and there. And I guess I feel safe at home. I am not sure the location matters, safety relies on my mental state. If I'm being honest, I don't feel safe with myself sometimes; so home is safe, I'm not. But only sometimes."

"So, how's your environment? Relationship with family? Friends? Yourself?"

"My family has been through a lot of hardship. My mom was diagnosed with cancer and she kept it from my family. My dad and sister were upset and blamed her for not telling them first. And then my mom fell out of liking with my dad, and my dad doesn't know. What's my relationship with my family? Lies. Deceit. Manipulation. To put it simply. Friends? I can't be entirely open with them because I've always been cautious on privacy, but I know they are there for me. I at times back into my little bubble of introversion and revel in my emotions away from them. It isn't good, I know. But I just can't do it sometimes. I feel tired. I'm not tired of them. I'm not tired of my family. I'm sort of tired of myself. It's my fault I fall for the lies, deceit, and manipulation. It's my fault I can't trust others. It's me. My relationship with myself? Unkind and unfair upon reflection, I suppose."

"Wait. Your mom lied about her cancer??"

Laughs on both sides. She talked to me like a friend instead of solely viewing me as a patient and I felt heard. She talked to me about my concerns and the things I was going through with sympathy but not pity. It felt like a breath of fresh air. We continued on with the conversation, but I consistently hid things from her. I couldn't help it. There were things I couldn't accept yet. I hadn't come to terms with it in my memory as real, so I couldn't reveal it. So I didn't. She had enough.

"So, OBVIOUSLY, you have depression." *Laughs on both sides.*

"So, now, I'm going to get your mom and we can discuss an agreement as to what to do moving forward."

I finally got to go home after about 4 hours in the hospital. I thought I would hgo in and leave with my form filled and the ability to go back to school. But I actually ended up going home with a more understanding mom, a therapist, a psychologist, and *an answer*. I guess the stay at the Hospital Hotel wasn't such a bad thing after all.

I'm still a little peeved about Dr. Murial going behind my back though.

Chapter 46

JUST TALK

I was sitting on a grey, kind of cushy couch with a pen in hand. Without a table, I leaned against the other cushion of the couch to hold the weight of my writing. Looking over to the far right of the paper, I added up the numbers:

Four.
Plus four more.
Plus three too.
Plus a questionable two too.

Totaling my score, I looked at the total: twenty-four. Twenty-four, marking my life for the 'very severe' category.

My mom woke me up this morning, and it was my first day to go in to talk to a stranger. A professional in the field of the mind, and someone who was supposed to help more than any school counselor, but worked essentially the same. Essentially the exact same, but instead of the repercussions happening at school, it was with my whole world. Instead of having the messing with just one component of my life, it has now bled over to everything else. I mean what am I supposed to even do when I walk in there? Talk? Please.

"I'm nervous…" I told my mom as we entered the office building.
"Why are you nervous?" My mom was treating this as a business
transaction to get one-and-done and leave as soon as
possible.

But I couldn't treat it that way. My mom was going in to try to
find an absolute, an ultimatum of sorts of a solution to my "crazy".
My "depression" apparently was now being forced to be helped by an
option to go to therapy. It felt more obligatory than therapy should
feel, but I figured it would probably just feel that way at first. Maybe,
I'll get something out of this. If not, this is really pointless. It'll be
fine. *Right?*

"I don't know. I guess I just don't know what is going to happen.
I'm nervous and I just hope that this helps and doesn't do
absolutely nothing."
"Honey, don't be nervous. It isn't something to be nervous about,
just talk."

Just talk. Never in my life have I ever found it easy to *just talk*
about my emotions, about apparently an important aspect of my life.
Why can't I just turn it off? Why can't I just return to the way I was,
an emotionless cyclone who couldn't process any form of emotion
coming my way? I mean I guess it has been beneficial for me to feel
and understand my friend's emotions so I can help them through
their mental health. But why can't I just turn it off for myself? I don't
need to feel? It's pointless and gets nothing done.
My mom walked through the hall in front of me; because similarly
to me, though she didn't want to admit it, she was antsy to get this
over with also. This was a foreign building, and the walls were red
bricks aligned in a manner that didn't have the feeling of comfort like
it should have. It felt more like a government building, providing the
exact opposite feeling. Today, I was supposed to see my psychiatrist.
A psychiatrist aid with medication and a therapist just talks to you

through your issues. Though different, both intimidated me equally. They were trying to make me *just talk.*

I stopped to look down at the business card my mom gave me prior that belonged to the psychiatrist and looked at the location of the room. My mom, on the other hand, kept walking and almost walked straight out of the building through another external door.

"Mommy." I belted after my mom with my voice in a brisk voice
    similar to a yell dipped in calm, "Stop."
My mom turned around, looked at me and awaited my opinion,
    "Calm down. Slow down. Take your time, and read the
    card. We go upstairs. Where are you going?"

Looking at me antsy and a bit embarrassed of herself for almost walking straight back outside with her head down, my mom laughed at herself and returned back to me. We clicked the elevator button and awaited the doors to open. My mom seemed more nervous than me, or more on edge anyways. I need to take on the calm one in this situation because she won't be.

The card stated, 'level 2 #221'. Translation: Second floor, room 221. *This is going to be a short ride.*

Ding. The doors opened and one foot in front of the other, we
    surely both ended up inside the elevator.
Da dum. Da dum. Oh, are we there already? Nope. That wasn't
    the elevator, just my heart trying to beat its way out of my
    chest to run out the doors even before the doors managed
    to close.
Clink. Second Floor.
Da dum. Da dum.

The elevator ride was quiet and full of angst on both my part and my mom's part. We couldn't bring ourselves to talk to each other because we both were experiencing the same nervous energy, but didn't want to talk about it. We didn't and couldn't. We both didn't want to show our true nervous feeling, and kept on our game faces, ready to approach the dragon.

> *brvvv.* The elevator slowly elevated upward towards the second
> floor. My stomach sank down to my feet and melted right
> on the floor, because of a mix between the movement
> against gravity and my nerves not being able to hold my
> guts in their places.
> I've got to keep my composure. *Breathe. For mommy.*
> *brvvv. cachunk.* The elevator came to a stop and the overhead
> number read '2'. I'm ready.
> *Ding.* The doors opened once more to reveal a new battleground,
> and my mom and I emerged onto the territory with our
> game faces on.
> "Mommy, I'm nervous."
> "Just talk."

We made our way to the door that read 221 and walked into the closed door. Past the door was the smallest waiting room I had ever seen; it resembled a cubicle without the desk, but instead, there was a couch and two waiting chairs along the wall. There was one large lamp hovering over the couches and on the wall was a painting of a lonely gray bunny rabbit. *I feel trapped.* This space is a little small for my comfort. There was another door further in the cube, and I assumed it led into the main war zone.

> "Do we go in?" I asked my mom because we both stood in the
> cube and it seemed that our time with enough oxygen
> was running out.

Without answering, my mother walked up to the door tensely and grabbed ahold of the doorknob. Without hesitation, she opened the door and we were met face to face with the jabberwocky. And suddenly in my hand, I felt the metaphorical sword I was fated to use to fend from this monster. My shield in front of me, we walked in after being welcomed by the psychiatrist.

She gestured towards the little white couch and my mom and I sat on it together. I sat straight up, posture composed like I was being held up to my promise of being the strong soldier in steel-metal armor. My mom, on the other hand, sat a person distance away from me on the couch in a slunched posture. This was my mom's fighting stance to fool her opponent into thinking she was off-guard, but truly, she was nervous. I could tell by her darting eyes and her lip biting. I took ahold of the conversation as the psychiatrist began her spiel.

"Welcome! My name is…" *let's say, Dr. Brazen.*
A head nod from my mom and me.
"So, from the case information your therapist has sent over to me and the case file's findings, I see that you have been diagnosed with depression." *No duh.*
"But I wanted to determine how depressed you are. Because, as you probably know, depression is on a scale and I want to figure out how depressed you are to figure out the best possible medication for you."
A head nod from my mom and me.
"Ok," an awkward smile from Dr. Brazen peered over her face, "so here is a paper test to determine where you are on the scale of depression. If you don't mind going out to the waiting room to take it, and I will stay in the room with your mom and discuss some things."
She handed me the paper packet.

I walked towards the door and left to enter the small waiting room again. The walls are thick and I am unable to hear the conversation outside of the little waiting room. I only see the couches and I feel trapped in my own mind. I was sitting on a grey, kind of cushy couch with a pen in hand. Without a table, I leaned against the other cushion of the couch to hold the weight of my writing. The paper test was composed of a variety of questions on the symptoms of depression. Basically, they were questions about my eating habits, my sleeping habits, my feelings, and it felt like one of the most cliche test paralleling to personality tests. I felt like I was filling out this test and felt a bit ashamed of the fact that a majority of these questions I related to. Maybe it was self-serving bias like on personality tests. I felt kind of cheap filling this out. When I finished, I looked over to the far right of the paper, I added up the numbers:

Four.
Plus four more.
Plus three too.
Plus a questionable two too.

Totaling my score, I looked at the total: twenty-four. Twenty-four, marking my life for the 'very severe' category. This feels so anticlimactic and makes me feel so cruddy as a person. Prior, I would assume that I would respond in shock and feel upset by how bad my depression is without realizing it before hand. However, I just didn't respond that way. I honestly didn't really care. 'It is what it is' was the mood I was in about this all. I truly solely had an urge to leave. I could easily leave out the first door and run home. It wasn't that far of a run. I would look more insane than my 'very severe' abnormality, but would I care? Not really. *Run. Run. Run.*

No, I shouldn't run, my mom is still here and I feel it wouldn't reflect well upon her if I just ran. My mom also needed me. She was on-edge and is only doing this for me. My superego was already working and running on the treadmill in my brain, I felt enough guilt to hold me down like chains in the couch resisting me from running home.

I'm done, should I go in? My mom and Dr. Brazen are talking, what if it is confidential and I shouldn't know about it? Do I just sit here? I can't run. I can't just walk in. I guess I just... *wait.*

At some point, Dr. Brazen came out to retrieve me.

"So you scored for 'very severe' depression" *I know, I counted it up for you.*

"Now, I suggest we prescribe something first to manage your sleeping habits, and then work on the medication for your depression."

The rest of the meeting felt like a fast forward movie, where I don't remember every detail anymore. I partially recall a one-on-one therapy session with my psychiatrist to determine what medication to do. I also remember taking a mouth swab to send in somewhere to figure out what medication would work best for my DNA. I honestly wouldn't know if they took my DNA to clone me or test to see if I am interesting of a phenomenon enough to study in research. Maybe one day I'll get snatched up for experiments on an extreme 'very severe' case of mental trauma, depression, anxiety, PTSD, and so many other issues embedded within me and my DNA. Who knows? I wouldn't be opposed, it seems kind of fun and would make me feel useful for my issues.

Chapter 47

THE WORST LIE OF ALL

Sometimes I think my family was doomed from the start, and somehow there was no chance we could have or even were ever a happy family. When I was little, I never thought about these things. I never worried that the imperfections that my family and my life had were anything of significance. But it hit me. I always knew. I was always prepared.

"I'm going to tell you something."

"Ok," she was my therapist, she shouldn't feel anxious to tell me something. She could easily just say it.

"And you may respond negatively, but I want you to respond honestly."

"Ok." My hands clenched between my thighs like I was trying to keep the circulation in my hands pumping from the cold shiver that circulated my whole body. Like frostbite numbingly putting me into shock of the fact I already knew.

"You have been depressed all your life."

Huh. Honestly, I'm not surprised at all. I thought I would be unhappy, respond negatively, blame others, lash out, or at least be in shock of something I could have never imagined would be the words to come out of her innocent lips that quivered in fear of hurting me. But no. In fact, I, on a certain level, felt relieved. Like finally, something didn't feel like a lie to me anymore. Like the deceptions, deceit, and duplicity were being stripped of its cover to reveal something I longed for. Ever have that moment when you knew something was true but never realized it till someone showed it to you or it became confirmed like a slap in the face by reality. I felt like I finally had to confront the worst lie of all with this new confirmation in my life. Interesting thing about lies actually...

Did *you* know the average person lies at **least** once or twice a day?

Ok, come on, don't feel *attacked.*

We *all* do it. To not *admit* you lie, you *actively* lie.

Some lies are to *purposely* deceive the *victims* of our words, others subconsciously as an adaptation of what is polite as our society has *established*, but the *worst* lies of all don't *fit* in either of these categories.

When *labeled* as a liar, you *are* frowned upon for life. You *are* untrustworthy, you *are* unfit. Then aren't we all *unfit*?

"HoW arE yOu DoiNg tOdaY?"

If you *answer* that you are doing well, are you *really*? Do you always *mean* what you say? Our society *has* established that it *is* polite to answer with a short brief answer that does not *cause* a lot of worry. A short answer that *satisfies* the question. A subconscious personal *adaption* to the question, *not* to the person, and especially *not* for yourself.

You *lied.*

You said you *were* okay, when you *weren't.*

No no, the lies that are done subconsciously as an adaptation of what is polite as our society has established is not the worst lie of all.

The worst *lie* of *all,*

is the *lie*

you tell yourself and actually believe.

The lie that you are not good enough. The lies you tell yourself about how you are a horrible person for a white lie that made no difference. That white lie you are feeling bad about is not as bad as the lie that you tell yourself that you don't deserve to be validated because of that white lie. The lie that you are wrong in thinking that something is wrong. The lie that you are okay.

Nothing could have been as bad. I never actively told myself I was normal. I never actively told myself that the things I was going through were for the usual folk. I just never actively wanted to believe otherwise. I couldn't bring myself to admit that maybe, just maybe, I've always just been depressed.

Chapter 48

WARY BELIEVER

My therapist told me to make a hope board. I was quite wary at first; not even just at first, I was just skeptical and still am of the whole idea and pushed it off. I ended up constantly seeing a flashing sign pop in my head throughout the days and weeks telling me to do it, but I just "accidentally" continued to "forget" to come around to it. Week after week, my therapist would pursue the hopeless idea of making me make one. *Haha, nope.* To that, I would emptily agree and promise to do it for the following week. A hope board is quite a simple concept, I admittedly never saw the point in things like that my entire life. I just never felt that they really had any value or could actually do anything.

When I was itty bitty, my sister, like most little impressionable girls who saw commercials of 'magical' girls who became so 'magical' through journals with pretty designs and locks and fluffy pens and puppy stickers with glitter, went through a diary phase.

THE DREADED DIARY PHASE.

Yes, you read that correctly. Every little girl running to their dads begging to get that one blue and pink journal with a lock because they saw it in a commercial and it made all the other little girls 'magical'. Then quickly being redirected to mom, the overseer of all 'major' purchases allowed in the house. With lots of gnawing, begging, and pleading; the little girl is finally able to convince the mom, like the little girl actually made a difference in swaying the mom's decision in putting money into a stack of papers in a binding, to allow the permission of getting this 'magic'-making diary. The story is always the same, every little early 2000s girl. The early 2000s' own version of the better 'American Doll' phenomenon spin on the story of a little girl who turned into a puppy princess with a binding of papers full of chalked up writing that isn't even legible years later.

I, as the younger sister, was dragged along on the journey. I was told to have a diary by my sister, and I was somehow strangled into convincing my parents of letting me have something I didn't even want in the first place like I truly longed for it for my whole itty bitty life thus far.

I. WROTE. NOTHING.

A majority of the journals/diaries, as I read back on it, was my sister's writing. She used to write about small 'pom-pom' characters in their own little royalty world of princes and princesses. Each character had their own love story, every princess had a prince. ***Bleh. I know.*** Putting my pride to the side for a second, I never told my sister, but I admittedly loved those diaries. Don't get me wrong, Princess Pink Flower Pom Pom depicted kissing her Prince Pink Pom Pom makes me so uncomfortable to see; and those stories weren't in any way entertaining with any plot of conflict but a simple childlike love story. ***Come in close. Closer. Shhhhhh…*** I used to read the stories when I was alone, sad, or in need of some comfort. I used to read the stories to solely adore the diary itself. The diary wasn't my diary, but it was. I didn't write anything, but it served its purpose for me because every time I read it, the only thing I saw was my sister's laugh, her voice reading it, her effort she put into it to express herself. Her happy face is the thing I read like braille whenever I cracked open those diaries to read the stories she had written for me. Reading her words made me have a weird cushy cozy feeling inside my chest. I felt the thing that can only be categorized as 'the happy'. It was a simple thing, I didn't even use it like most believers in the ability of the diaries, but I got my 'magical' moment. My 'magical' moment was seeing the twinkle in my sister's smile as I sat and enjoyed the stories of the 'Pom Pom Princess Twins and Their Pom Pom Princes' because of that smile. I don't believe in things like diaries, journals, and hope boards to bring happiness or hope; but it did do its job no matter how much of a fight I put up against it.

You'd think that I'd learn to blindly trust these kinds of devices that are supposed to aid in my happiness; but when has any human being ever learned anything with just one mistake? Of course, I have to do it again. *DUH.*

I put off the hope board for several weeks. I stopped writing all together of my own personal words for years. I ended up not making a hope board, *YOU THOUGHT!* But I did end up getting the same effect. I made a collage of a whole bunch of old and current photos to decorate my desk. But I soon found myself feeling an overwhelming sense of that same feeling of 'the happy' and a new sense: Hope. I look up every time I sit there, and I smile. I see the smile I had in those photos and I see the smiles of others. I hear the laughter of every memory and hear the final piece in the buzzing of the voices in my head telling me everything wrong. I feel the tension in my face from all the smiling, and most of all, I feel the happiness I felt with all of those moments, people, and feel grateful to have that final taste of hope I never thought I would get the luxury to taste.

I'm Skeptical. I am Cynical. And I don't believe, to say the least. But I am

The Wary Believer.

Chapter 49

SCREAM

" **W**hat the hell is wrong with you?" my sister finally noticed I was crying.

Trying to let out a peep, even a small one, I can't. *Frozen.*

"You have no right to just act like something is wrong, cry in my car, and lie to me. You can't just do that. Now tell me, what is wrong."

Like a noose around my neck, my claws clinging to my throat like I could puncture a hole to finally release the tension. The pressure of the breath, air, blank spaces of importance, and word vomit pressing up against my vocal cords. My thoughts banging on the door, screaming to be let out of their own prison. Every instinct in my body aggressively rings the broken doorbell trying to hint on my body's need to share. I want to scream, but my mouth doesn't open. I want to scream, but the key to the lock has been swallowed inside the enclosed cage. Ever think your brain overthinks with an overflowing of butterflies and bats? They both instinctively know they have a common goal to escape, but they turn against each other.

Fighting, killing, blood, splatter. Scratching up and killing the inside. All knowing the solution was simple: open your mouth.

She stopped the car. Parked. Letting out a large gust of air out of the depths of her lungs, releasing nothing but hot air.

Just Open Your Mouth. You are fine, nothing happened. Stop it.

Feeling her energy releasing over to me, I know she hates me. She hates me. She blames me. She is angry at me. Why am I causing that? *Stop it. Stop whatever is making her angry. Stop everything. Just stop whatever she doesn't like.*

"We aren't going home until you answer me," my sister angrily grunts out.

My mind running races, I can't breathe. Just

Focus Focus Focus
Just Focus
Loss of focus
All too familiar for me
I can't go back
A feeling of depression
Depressed, stressed, but so much less
I feel panicked
Lacking focus
Stressed out of my mind
Lots on my plate
But unable to breathe through it all
Ugh
Focus Focus Focus
Just Focus
At least

Ok. Figure out what's going on. *Breathe. Focus.*

My sister must be really angry at me.

Ok, analyze the situation. Just do that first. What happened? Retrace your steps. What did I do today? *Breathe. Focus. You can do this.*

She must hate me.

Focus. You can't make her feel better unless you figure out how to tell her nothing is wrong and prove it. Cause nothing is wrong. *Focus.* Prove it. What did I do today?

*   *   *

The warmth of the sun melted my cold daze away. My eyes slowly popped open like two blooming flowers, allowing me to see my morning lit ceiling. Laying in my bed, I didn't feel inclined to move yet. Mornings are hard for me.

Something about the simple act of just getting up is difficult. Dragging my body out of bed, my depression, like a bag of rocks, dragging me down. Numbingly, I've done this a million times before; knowing full well, I still have to force it. I still have to force myself out of bed, even though every nerve, muscle, and thought in my body protests in disdain. *Get up!*

I remember thinking to myself, it will get easier one day. it will feel blissful again one day to wake up, instead of hoping I just died in my sleep to avoid this inner battle. *Click. EeeEee. Thud.*

The door to my room opened wide. With an unlocking click, my ears intuitively knew to warn the rest of my body to prepare for a fight. The door slowly creaked and then briskly opened and hit the wall with a thud loud enough to slam the door knob straight through the wall. My body responded to my ear's warning and quickly pulled my body straight up, engaging every muscle in my back into its rightful place. *God, I'm sore.*

"HIIIIIII THÀNHHH!" my sister burst into my room screeching.

Thành is my Vietnamese name. In America, Thành is my middle name; but culturally, Thành is actually my first name in Vietnam. The real question is which one do I identify with and what it says

201

about me. When asked my name, I always answer, "Wynn Thành Phi". It isn't that I am not proud of my Vietnamese culture, it's just that I live in the United States. The name often used to refer to me is Wynn, or sometimes just Phi. I adore just Phi. I love Phi. Phi reminds me of the family unit and one of my core values. I adore family and for me it is one of my top priorities in my list of responsibilities. I feel obligated to my family and the last name Phi makes me feel that way. Family values are a cultural thing for Vietnamese people and also for Buddhists, which I am. Thành Phi, to me, has no cultural significance; it just suits me I think. But Thành. Thành means so much. It means successful. I don't believe that. More like an angel meant for success given to my parents that fell from the sky instead of being granted, basically a Lucifer. Anyways, Thành is my home name. My family only refers to me as Thành, and I respond immediately and much faster than when referred to as Wynn by my friends.

"Thành, are you busy today?" my sister presses on me.

"Yes and no. Why? What do you want?" I always say the same thing every time. It honestly is because I know no matter what my sister asks, I'll try my best to do it for her despite whether I have work. She is more important.

"Want to go to the mall with me today? I need to go buy gifts for my friends and I don't want to go alone!"

No. "Sure."

This is clearly something she can do on her own. Why am I going? It's fine though, because I know my sister has a need to be around people 24/7. My sister and I ended up being opposites that way. My sister is an extreme extrovert who gets depressed when alone and is pushy, demanding to get her way; and I am an extreme introvert who spends the majority of her time alone but has become accustomed to learning to be an extrovert because I am lenient with my sister. *Toxic relationship?* TBD.

"Get dressed! Hehe, I want to look cute!"

I just get up and start going. Okay, I guess. I wasn't sure what cute meant today. Everyday my style seems to shift to compensate for my ever-shifting, fluid depression and whatever ails me that day.

*   *   *

"PUT DOWN YOUR PHONE, AND TALK TO ME!" my sister started to yell now.

I realized I was looking at my phone, panicking in every 42 facial muscles. Hyper focused on the black screen on my phone, but my mind in another universe trying to find some solace in the focus I couldn't seem to find.

  God. She probably wants to kill me, and I'd understand.

Wait, wait, *Focus.* Ignore her, you know you need to get your head straight first before you can lie through this situation like nothing is wrong.

Focus.

Focus.

Focus.

*   *   *

What did I wear? Well, I ultimately decided to wear my camouflage cargo pants with a million pockets that I love, a grey workout turtleneck, and a camouflage jacket that matched the pants. I remember being kind of proud of it. I felt like a badass, that felt like a sadass inside. I was ready to go.

The car ride was agonizing. My sister kept talking in circles about her indecisiveness as to what to get her one male friend that she liked. It was like none of her other friends' gifts didn't matter because she'd wing it and find something. No questions about me or even noticing that I just wasn't in the mood to be able to answer her questions.

Just on and on about, "what type of wallet do you think he'd like? This one or this one? Louis Vuitton or Gucci? Or maybe this one? Help me decide, please?"

"I don't know. I don't like Gucci, I think maybe Louis Vuitton if you want to get him a brand name," I responded in a monotone voice like a computing computer.

I've never really liked brand names. I have nothing against them, and I have nothing against people who buy brand names, it's just not for me. Ever since I was little, I used to go shopping with my whole family a lot. Our little family unit of Dad, Mom, Sister, and Me. My sister wanted to buy everything, she had a sense of style. I had none, so often I'd tag along to just watch. My mom did the same, but at the time, my sister would go with my mom and I would go with my dad. My dad would look at the items my sister wanted to buy and judge it for every strand of fabric. "These shoes will hurt your feet after a while", "this fabric is not good", "this bag is too expensive for the quality", and just "no"'s were all I heard echoing in my little head whenever we went shopping. You know how people say when you walk into a Target, you always end up coming out with more than you anticipated? Ya, my family always ended up leaving with less than anticipated, with money still in our pockets. I grew up with that and obtained that quality. I don't like to spend loads of money on things unless I pre-examine the quality of the product, the durability, the usage, and the future usage. Therefore why I personally don't buy brand names. They are EXPENSIVE, and also all products I wouldn't use a lot in the future. Not worth it in my mind, but if my sister wants to spend money on that, not my call.

"Ya, but I know him, he might like Gucci," my sister counter argued.

If she knew, why did she ask? "Ok."

And on and on it went. My sister repeated the same spiel of confusion as to what to do for a gift for that one male friend, as I sat in the passenger seat with my whole body still tense and regretting saying sure to going. My sister does this a lot. She is quite indecisive about everything, and often asks questions cyclically until she comes to a conclusion. She may be asking questions, but the reality, is that despite what you say she comes to a conclusion on her own. However, you are obligated to give an answer anyways because she needs that interaction and affirmation despite deciding on her own.

We made it to the mall and the venture began. I felt like I was being dragged along like a cat being forced to go on a walk like a dog and didn't want to in the first place. *Uh Oh.*

"Omg, I need more bras. Do you need anymore? Can we go? Let's go," my sister and I approached the corner where Victoria's Secret stood.

I have never been able to walk into this store without having trouble breathing. Now that I think about it, I guess that means it's a trigger. I feel always so uncomfortable walking into these stores and something about it makes my soul want to sprint out of my body like running the 10,000 metre race. I really don't want to do this today. My mind started to scatter. My eyes darted around and my stomach felt like it was crumbling into my bladder. My lungs started to palpitate in sync with my now fast beating heart.

"Do you need to do resizing?" there was a woman standing at the front of the store that wouldn't let us through without answering this question. *NOOOO. I can't!* Not a word came out of my mouth. "No, we are sized up to date," my sister answered calmly and cheerily. Walking in.

*　　*　　*

"THÀNH, DID YOU HEAR ME?! PUT. DOWN. YOUR. FUCKING. PHONE. TELL ME WHAT THE HELL IS WRONG!" my sister scolded me.

I came back to reality, my mind was still racing and scattered. I can't breathe. I CAN'T breathe. I CAN'T BREATHE. Panic overtook my body. The already tense muscles in my whole body began to tremor with anxiety.

Focus. Just put down the phone. That's what she wants. Just do it. DO it!

My fingers frozen in place but my hands trembling, my phone flipped out of my hand without the grace I had hoped for. It was more like a fish vigorously flipping out in its final moments of life in the dryness of the air.

"Oh my god. Are you acting out right now? Chill."

I couldn't speak, now all I could focus on was my frustration. That fuming and internal flame growing inside my chest and burning up to my nose. I couldn't breathe, I just felt angry. I felt angry, frustrated, upset, and, most of all, out of control. I noticed my hands were shaking intensely. Or was it just my head? Everything was tremoring, my whole body was going into panic and shock. I couldn't stop.

"What's happening? Thành?!"

"I'm having a **panic attack!**" I pushed out with the best of my ability. Bad decision. My breath started to strip and shorten into milliseconds. It started to hurt. It was like I started to experience extreme dyspnea for pushing out the big gust of air just to say that one phrase this whole time.

"Well, I know that. What can I do? I don't know how to handle this."

No, duh. My whole body was shaking still, and my hands had it the worst. Usually, my hands have a natural tremor due to anxiety. This time it added onto it and it was just spazzing out. I tried my best to try to control it.

No wait, that's not right. What am I supposed to do in this situation? *Think. Think. Focus. Thành, Focus.* What do you do for a panic attack, despite this one being the worst one I've ever had? *Focus on breathing.* That is all I have to do. Focus on breathing. Don't get frustrated within yourself for not being able to breathe, just focus on the fact you are breathing. *Just breathe. Breathe. BREATHE GODDAMMIT!*

My sister tried to hold my hand in that very moment and my hand briskly whisked her hand away. I couldn't be touched. Don't touch me. Just don't see me. Don't. Just don't.

She must hate me. I'm scaring her.
Stop scaring her, it's all your fault.
Just stop it.

Stop, I need the world to stop. I need to calm down. I did nothing wrong. *Breathe.* Slow down your breathing and make the breaths longer. It's okay. Just relax. You did nothing wrong.

Curling. My body started to churn inwards and I went into my survival position. My head tucked between my legs and my hands hugging the back of my neck. My whole body is just so tense. I narrowed my focus to hugging my neck, and allowed my body to breathe. Suddenly, I felt a light touch of my sister's gingerly fingers touch my back trying to pat the life back into me. I breathed in a big gulp of air and pressed out another phrase, "don't touch me." My sister quickly removed her hand and said, "I'm sorry, I don't know what to do. Do you want to go home? Do you want me to open the window? Do you want to step outside? What do you need?" *Dingus, I can't answer.* I wasted my breath on the simple 'do not touch me'. I couldn't see her, but I could just feel her eyes staring at me with the worst feeling possible: pity. *Can you just forget about me? That's what I need.* "I'm going to go home. But, I need you to lift your head upright for me to do that," I could just hear the pity in every syllable that exited my sisters mouth. Ok, next mission: lift your head and don't go backwards in your progress through this panic attack. After a few minutes of finally breathing somewhat normally (I forgot what my normal breathing was like so I just assumed), I slowly lifted my head into the upright position and kept my hands hugging my neck.

My sister drove me home.

Recovery occurred after that, and I honestly didn't want to talk about what had just happened with my sister. It might have been because immediately after I just started to recover, she said to me, "I'm sorry, I didn't know what to do. Tell me what I can do, because *I* don't know what it feels like".

Chapter 50

'GOOD'

I don't consider myself necessarily religious in any way. Some people find comfort in religion and in looking to a higher power, allowing their beliefs that this higher power has a plan for them ahead that reflects the light. Coming from a Buddhist family, I have not strayed from the values taught to me by Buddhism and by my family. However, I have strayed a bit to understand my own beliefs and understandings of my spirituality. I generally believe there are otherworldly powers in play in my life and in the world, and I must sit and fight my own demons. I have to fight them to reach a level of enlightenment. There is no belief to blindly believe everything will turn out well because I am blindly following, worshipping, or am a devoted follower to my religion; but instead, there is acknowledgment that my life will surpass its hardships, but that should not sway me on my ability to be true to being a good person. Am I a good person? I am only human, so there is no way for me to consistently and constantly be a 'good' being per se, but even a human can reach enlightenment.

According to the origins of Buddhism, Buddha was a man. Born to a king, Prince Siddhartha Gautama was born under a prophecy: he would either become a powerful tyrannical king or become a great spiritual leader. At the time, there was a religious questioning throughout the people, who at the moment followed Hinduism. Hinduism prophesied that our lives are a continuous cycle of karma, where in the next life our karma would determine what we came back as and would determine our fate for that life until we paid back that karma as a 'good' person. His father, the king at the time, feared that Siddhartha would be subjected to the second fate, so he kept him isolated and stowed away from the world in their castle. After 29 years of that, Siddhartha sneaked out to see the people. He came across the Four Signs: an aged man, a sick man, a dead man, and a religious ascetic. Through these signs, Siddhartha came to a rude awakening that he, too, could become old, sick, dead, and lose everything. Siddhartha came to the conclusion that the way he believed life to be was a trickery that he realized actually was just an unending cycle of suffering from wants and losses. Siddhartha left home and followed the life of a religious ascetic, to try to attain a sense of being and purpose and to escape the cycle. Failing to do so, he finally stopped and sat beneath a tree and went through the tests of life. He was subjected to the sins and cravings of life in his spiritual awakening and came out the other end enlightened and the Buddha.

There are a lot of details to the legend that I don't necessarily feel entirely convinced by, however, to me, the ending, is the most important. From a cynical viewpoint, I don't believe that the sins came to bother the Buddha in physical forms; but instead, I do believe that the Buddha had to go through those hardships in his life in order to reach that point where he was a 'good' and enlightened person. I believe there are other-worldly powers at play that put our lives in positions of hardship and in positions of happiness, but the important part is that you are able to sustain your good nature despite it all. Spiritually, I feel that the lessons taught in Buddhism have weight and meaning in a way that seems legitimate. Our world is full of evils, and there is no promise that they won't happen because of a belief in a higher power; but instead, you have to fight to reach the end. Never stop fighting to be a good person, because that enlightenment can defeat your karma and you won't have to repeat life to fulfill that.

I have been subjected to many hardships in my life, in a way that does not resemble anyone else exactly, and that was the fate I was to be subjected to. I don't complain or blame others for it because, at the end of it all, I'll come out a better person for it. If the others involved don't, I can't help them. I can only look forward and stay a good person who helps other people through hardship and give back to the world in the way I always wished others would do for me. People go seeking good people to become acquaintances with, and some people become overwhelmed and obsessed with finding them. That obsession rarely ends with the ability to find someone who is a genuinely kind person who knows you better than you know yourself and is the purest form of genuine friendship. Those 'good' people who are kind without exception are rare to find. Some people search all their lives and never find them. I had lost hope in ever finding someone good to be friends with or lean upon. In those dark times, I felt alone and could not, would not, and let not myself be vulnerable enough with anyone to feel otherwise. Instead, I have found myself believing that if I can't find someone like that, I'll try my best to be the next best thing. I will try my best to be that 'good' person for others. In no way am I preaching that I am the definition of a 'good' person, but I try my best to follow the footprints of Buddha, and despite my hardships, stride forward and help others. I would never hope or imagine my life to align with the journey of the Buddha; but I do hope that, at the end of it, I know that I did my best to avoid repeating the same mistakes and feelings afflicted upon me and positively pay it forward.

I honestly don't know anything about the beliefs of the afterlife for Buddhism, except that if you reach enlightenment you can escape the cycle presented in Hinduism. But, in traditional Asian culture, there are quite a few traditions surrounding the idea of the afterlife. As someone originating from Vietnamese culture, I can only attest and speak to that.

Growing up, my parents were split on their beliefs allowing me to basically pick-and-choose my own adventure. My dad grew up with no beliefs, no traditions, and no parental figures. Don't get me wrong, my grandparents on my dad's side are alive and well; but they were never the parenting sort and treated their children in the traditional hierarchy: 1. Elders, 2. Adults, 3. Children/Workers. That was the only tradition they kept in their family, but they had no beliefs otherwise. My dad believes that once you are deceased, you are gone. Death is the ultimatum. My mother, on the other hand, grew up with a strong relationship with religion and it can be seen through my aunt, her sister. My aunt believes in every single detail of the origination and beliefs of Buddha. When my mother was young, in fourth grade approximately (school worked differently in Vietnam in comparison to America), she lost her mother to death. My grandma is someone I view as somewhat of a guardian angel. Every year, we welcome and celebrate her coming to visit us from the afterlife on her memorial day and on Lunar New Year. On those days, we lay out traditional foods, delicacies, sweets, and other yummy dishes we cook. Along with this we light incense and place flowers, fruits, and beautiful things around the altar, where her beautiful picture resides perfectly in the center. Traditionally, there are two altars, one for Buddha and another for the ancestors. Per family, you can place pictures for different ancestors you welcome home from your family tree; but for my family, we stick to just my grandma.

My grandmother was a wonderful woman and someone I truly wish I could have met during this lifetime. She was kind and soft-spoken, but she learned the importance of standing up for herself, her values, and those she loved. Though she was so sweet and blooming like a flower, she had a cheeky side of jokes, pranks, and a sense of humor anyone would like. She was lovable, like a blooming flower. You couldn't help but just look at her in awe of her greatness. She loved her family and loved life as everyone wishes they could. Her husband, my grandpa was a Chinese General, and his relationship with my grandma was illegal. The government officials were after him, and to protect his family, he left. He left before my mother was old enough to know him or remember him. My grandma was left alone to care for the pieces left behind. She cared for my aunt, my uncle, and my mom with all her heart and never felt any sense of resentment against my grandpa; she just... Loved.

She knew her time was coming, but she didn't want to leave the life and family she loved. Life was something she wanted to fight for, but she knew she couldn't and didn't have a choice. My mom told me a story about the last few moments where my grandma was still with us.

She said to my aunt, uncle, and my mom, "My time is coming. Death is not something you should resent, and I don't want you to stop living when I'm gone. You will grow up and make lives of yourselves, I know it."

She looked at my aunt, "You will grow up and work hard and fulfill a life as a doctor. You will live independently and you will make me so proud as you fulfill a full life even without me."

"Honey, you will also become a doctor. You will marry a woman and have a full house of pittering feet. 3 kids. I will look upon you and know that I am proud of you," she said to my uncle.

"I love you," my mom was crying as my grandma looked upon her and continued on, "and you, my precious girl, you will become a dentist. A successful one at that. And you will lead a life with many hardships. You will have two beautiful girls and a reluctant husband. But please learn to love your life."

"I love you all, and I'm sorry I can't stay. I wish I could, but life will pull me in a different direction in my path of life. I'm sorry. I'll always be here for you, and any time you need help, I'll be here," she hugged them tightly in her arms, clinging to the hope she could stay there forever, "I'll always be here."

She was right. The fates of my aunt, uncle, and mother ended up the way she prophesied. Each one of them forgot about the remarks of my grandma until years later when they had already come true. This is one of the reasons why I truly believe my grandma was an angel brought to earth but taken back. Just like that, she was *gone*.

My mom thinks I'm insane. I know when she reads this she will make a face and laugh at my imagination. But I loved my grandma and love her more than anyone knows. I've never met her, but I talk to her. I pray to her. I love her. Most of all, I miss her. She brought me my mom, made a sacrifice that shaped my mom to be who she is, and let me not lose her. She protects my mom in ways I can't describe. I owe her my life in ways.

When I was younger, my sister prayed and talked to my grandma more than I did. I didn't form a strong relationship with her early on like my sister did, or at least I thought. I wasn't old enough to form my own beliefs and I didn't want or desire much; and the way my sister prayed made me believe she was doing it the only right way. My sister would talk to my grandma about winning math competitions, getting good gifts, and her materialistics hopes in life. I figured my sister's method was the only correct one, and since I didn't want any of those things and didn't want to ask her to go out of her way to help me, I didn't talk to her much. I didn't really want to bother my grandmother with things I really don't need and I decided to allow myself to subject the fate given upon me instead of asking for better times. I wanted to give my sister the ability to ask for what she wanted and have my grandma focus on her, and I didn't want to steal the limelight. As a kid, I never truly believed in Santa Claus, the Tooth Fairy, or any other gift-giving, out-of-this-world being. I mostly didn't believe in them because I didn't want anything. When it came time to get gifts, I wouldn't have a list. I'd just ask for the same thing everytime: "I wish my family and friends are happy and healthy. Just make sure they are all okay".

I don't know what my mother talked to my grandma about, but she would sometimes spend hours on end just talking and praying. I hope she gets all she hopes for. I hope she's happy. And I hope my grandma gives her the life she deserves and I can manage to keep myself out of trouble enough to make her proud.

As years passed, my sister and I both entered high school. The

Lunar New Year prior to my freshman year, I asked my grandma to hope I do well my first year in highschool to get as much done as possible, and make it out the other end successful. Accomplished.

I did. I came out of the year with victory in my academics and school work, but, unlike usual, I also had a few more visits with my grandma. I finally had something to ask her for: *let me keep my mom.* My mom told my family she had cancer, and said she had already had it for two years already. I felt no resentment towards her for not telling me, but I did feel helpless. It was out of my control. But this was the first time I ever truly wished for something so badly that I felt desperate enough to bother my grandmother for once. I was scared. Terrified. And this was something I knew I couldn't handle alone, let alone if my mom ended up... *no, stop.*

We made it home after our annual Christmas trip to Austin, after my mom dropped the bomb the morning of my Grandmother's birthday. That was a long 2-3 hour drive of taciturn. But when we got home, the opening of the house front door immediately cued the yelling, avoidance, ignorance, and divergence. I just stood there and seeped it all in like the absorbance of a sponge until I sagged and felt my soul drown in the flooding of emotions. There is no helping us. There is no solution. For once, I've felt like we needed some extra aid. Not for me, my dad, nor for my sister; but for my mom. I abruptly went to get out of everyone's way and put my belongings in their rightful places, their normal places. And then shifted my weight to my heart and followed it up the stairwell to go see my grandma on the altar. My parents had retreated and left home to go "work" at their separate clinics on paperwork, and my sister retreated to our room to FaceTime one of her friends to 'spill the tea'. I went to the small room in the far corner of the first hall upstairs, and entered the safest place I know. So alone but not.

Usually, on Lunar New Years and on my grandma's memorial, I happily and excitedly volunteer to camp out outside the little small room to make sure the incense doesn't run out. The incense is the way for my grandma to stay in the physical world and enjoy the meal we provide. Whenever we want to ask her to come back, we just have to light an incense and ask the gods to allow her to come back. Usually, I play a game with my grandma. It sounds so weird and strange as I'm typing this out, but it is true. Every time, I always lay out a pillow and a sleeping bag on the floor outside the doorway. I would have homework and would sit there and do it. I'd play nice soft calming music, as to not disturb her visit with ruckus. I would light the incense and ritually pray to welcome her, and then go about my business of laying on the ground doing homework. I at times would read my book out loud to her and talk to her silently as I lay there. My sister, my dad, or my mom would sometimes walk up to add more foods to the altar and see me speaking aloud to her. *A giggle.* That was the usual response because my mom thinks it's cute that I have that kind of happiness with my grandma, and my dad and sister would think I'm ridiculous. My sister at this point stopped believing, speaking to, and truly caring about whether or not my grandma would come back. I think her life just... moved on. I used to think my sister was everyone's, including my grandma's, favorite but now I think, this might be my chance to change that. I just want to show her I love her. Nothing more. Nothing less. Just, I love her. Every few moments, I would have an eerie feeling that I can't describe fully. But it kind of feels like a pulling of my attention, an internal cry to me, and a kind remark trying to grab my attention. Instinctually and immediately, I peep through the doorway to always amazingly see that the incense is running out. It always amazes me. My grandma has never spoken a word to me or given me an evidence driven sign, but we have our own way of communicating and playing games. I think she might just love me.

I came to my grandma that day not from a place of joy, fun, and games; but now it was just in need of support. I find it hard to ask for help from anyone and hate to admit vulnerability, but I needed someone. And I know my grandma knows that the way I am and what I need: just someone to solely and simply listen for me.

Crrr-Schlick. I lit up the lighter and began to start up the incense. Placing one on the altar for Buddha and one for my grandma, I begged Buddha to allow me a few moments with my grandma. And turned to speak to her. Generally, when praying I stand out of respect, but after the beginning ritualistic prayers I just fell to the ground and looked upon her endearing face with tears running.

"Bà, are you there?"...

*I need someone right now. I don't want to be selfish, and I don't want to cause trouble... err more trouble. I really don't. I just don't know what to do. Bà, please help me. Mommy has cancer. Cancer. You probably already knew, mommy probably already told you before us. If she told anyone, she'd tell you. I'm glad she had you in her corner for those definitely grueling two years. Without anyone to help her. All alone. In excruciating pain physically from treatment and from her body betraying her mind. And on top of that, lasting judgement on her weight loss. Why couldn't people just let her be? Why didn't she feel safe enough to tell anyone? I guess I get it. I redact the question. Everyone's judgey, stressful, talkative, and worst of all, suffocating. I get it. I don't resent her decision to keep it hidden. I would do the same, and it was for the better. I guess I just feel helpless in knowing she had to go through it alone, and even now. Daddy is mad at her for not telling him because he is her husband and should know. No mention and no hint of concern for her well-being. Phung (my sister's Vietnamese name) is just going on and on about how her life is ruined because her mother has cancer and now must share **her** pain with her friends. Mommy is alone still... well, not alone, she has you. That's what I wanted to actually ask you about... I know I don't ask for much because I hate to bother you, but can I be selfish this once? Can you make sure mommy is okay? She's healthy? You don't have to force her to talk to me about it, I want her to feel comfortable and safe in her privacy; just can you make sure... make sure... make sure she... stays? I... I can't lose her. Please. Please, I am not as strong as she was. When she lost you, she grew from it and became a strong, independent woman who endured so much to give me a life that she never had. But, I'm not ready. I'm not even close to ready. Please. Bà, please. Let me keep her.*

The incense ran out. And my tears dried up, because as years passed my mom fought through the cancer as a warrior would. My grandma pulled through and I thank her everyday for letting my mother stay with me. Never have I ever loved and missed someone so much that I have never met.

Approximately two years later, my grandma received another visit from me. This one was absolutely unexpected to me; but probably not for her. I had just gotten back from my trip to California, and immediately went upstairs to see her the minute I came home.

"Hi, Bà, it's me again."

I know you know what happened. I have no words and can not accept it still, I feel tired. I feel wrong. I feel dirty. Bà, I feel like I have so many regrets over it. Bà, I really wish you were physically with me right now. I wish you could hold me and cleanse me of this consuming and overbearing feeling. I feel tingly down there, and I feel my brain squeezing all of the oxygen out. I just want to end it all. I want to die more than I have ever in the past. I could handle my internal issues before and feelings of 'depression', if that even is what it is; but I don't know about this. I'm scared. I should have just called mommy. I should have just called her. Why didn't I? Maybe I would feel better now. No, I did the right thing. She isn't further bothered and I didn't cause more issues for the family. I am not a bother because I'm keeping it to myself. Sorry for bothering you. I don't even know what I needed from talking to you. I don't know what happened. I could have done something. It's my fault. Bà, I don't know if I did the right thing. I don't know if... if I'll survive this. Can you help me? If it's my time, let me go easily and let the transition for Mommy and Phung to be easy? Allow the let go of my friends with ease. Let them all move on like I never existed. My disgusting trash self didn't deserve to be alive so just let it be like I never existed. Please? Or, if it isn't my time, help me know, if ever, when I should tell someone about it? I just can't decipher right from wrong alone. Clearly. If I could this would never have happened. Please help guide me through this. I know we don't talk and me asking this may be asking a lot, but if not that, just hug me through it. I don't have mommy, and I just... I just... just need someone to hold me.

I fell asleep there curled up in a ball in the corner on the floor closest to my grandma's altar. She held me and patted me into blissful sleep like a guardian angel.

Chapter 51

MIGRAINE

Squeezing, wheezing, and gasping for air.

Migraines are the worst. It feels like my brain is being suffocated by my own skull. The human skull is meant to give structure and protect our constructively destructive minds, that apparently need the protection from the world. So why does it feel like my skull is letting out every last bit of freedom inside?

My brain is squeezing.

A constructively destructive mind is what all humans own. Our minds build us up to build the best forms of ourselves. We seek perfection. But that exact thing destroys our civilization and our individual lives. We promote ourselves but sabotage our health. It isn't healthy to constantly feel

a squeeze.
To constantly feel
a wheeze.
To constantly feel
our brains are gasping for air,
because the thing suffocating us is not just our
own skulls,

It's our mind.
But maybe, just maybe…
The basis of my migraine is
My Overthinking.

Chapter 52

MY BAD HABIT

"I care for myself. The more solitary, the more friendless, the more unsustained I am, the more I will respect myself."
— **Charlotte Brontë, Jane Eyre**

I have quite a number of flaws. However, if I did a group vote of everyone who knows me and all the voices in my head, they would all agree that my top biggest flaw is my big bad habit: *I run.*

I have come to understand the things I go through are inevitable and I will accept them wholeheartedly because it is my truth. I have gone through my life believing that there are things I can't control that will succeed at putting me in a box and label me as something that I am not or I refuse to want to be. That I ultimately relent and accept. It's hard to believe that I could be more than all I've known to be and to be with people who have always been with me. The truth is you need to grow. The truth is I need to grow. The truth is that I... I want to grow.

I want to leave the world that I have known behind and start anew, because the things that I know are ones that have sewn so deep into who I am that it's starting to hurt. The stitches trying to bond me together are now pulling and straining because the muscles in my body jerk towards freedom.

I want to run.

And when I begin to run towards growth and away from the problems that I used to have, those stitches pull and pull and rip holes into my body; leaving behind shards of the way I used to be in a place that I used to be in.

But now I can run.

I can be free.

I can run away.

Galloping away like the gazelle running away from his home going to greener pastures, but sadly going damaged. *I don't wanna be damaged.* I just don't want to.

In order to be who I am today, the thing is that I had to be subjected to it all to become a new damaged version of myself. Is it better? Was I really running to greener pastures or was it all an illusion because there is a part of me, like a child, still needs hope? Being forced to grow up so early on in my life, I have never ever felt like I could just be a child. Never feeling the purest form of happiness every child experiences at the beginning of their lives. Did I go to a better place or did I just run away from one that I didn't like anymore? Did I leave one behind because I couldn't handle it anymore?

I ran into a void.

I really just delved into the unknown because the unknown seemed safer for some reason. I ran into the void to avoid the reality of my emotions and trauma and left behind the stitches, structure, safety, flesh, and bones. I left damaged: holes torn from my heart, scorch marks on my mind, and weight on my soul. I left because it was somehow better. It somehow felt safe. I didn't feel restrained and I didn't feel overwhelmed by manipulation wallpapering the box I was placed in. I ran to a void, wall-less and stainless.

Run.

I have now formed a habit. Anytime I feel myself getting too close to someone or someone is growing an attachment or a dependence upon me, I squirm. My body jerks at the horizon of responsibility for someone else's emotions, trying to resist the net that they have thrown over me to keep me. My heart screams to resist the inevitable pain that could occur for me or for them. My throat closes like a noose is trying to keep me unresistant. Instinctually…

I run away.

What is a habit? A habit is a "settled or regular tendency or practice, especially one that is hard to give up" according to the dictionary. But what does that mean? A habit is comfort. A habit is easy. A habit is a tendency that is formed and kept because it is easier and more comfortable to keep it. My bad habit is that I run away. Because of how my family and others in my life manipulated me into feeling responsible for them and they could feel fully dependent upon me emotionally, mentally, and, sadly, physically; I run. I've learned to run. Any time anything feels even remotely close to someone wanting me to be there for them, I run. Any time I feel like I could get sucked in because I care too much, I run. I leave before they can leave me. I leave before I feel that way again. I leave before I feel like my life will circle back.

I run for MY life.

Where do I run to? I run to the void or I run to someone else. I leave towards a place where I don't feel responsible, a place where I can just be a child, a place where I can just leave behind my life outside the door. I run to Bailey Haer.

I run towards her.

Bailey Haer is by no means my emotional support. I am quite private about my life and so I don't tell Bailey Haer anything about my depression, my family, or otherwise. Bailey Haer, to the outside eye, may seem like a bad friend to me; but she isn't. She is perfect. She isn't there for me through the depression, she is there for me in coping. She isn't there for me through the drama and mental health of my life, but she is there for me to bring me a little light in the dark without even needing to know what is in my shadow. I have come to a place of habit to run to her whenever I want to drop off the planet. She automatically shows up with a rocket ship and we travel to the moon and explore new worlds together. Laughing our heads off and like without gravity, we float. I float.

I float away from my problems. Weightless.

Running away may be my bad habit, and it hurts a lot of people's feelings; but how can it be so bad if I get to *float* weightlessly for the first time in my life?

   … it is a little *selfish*, I guess…

Chapter 53

DON'T LEAVE

Please don't leave me.
Don't deceive me.
Don't treat me like a sheet
A paper you write on and leave.

Marked for life,
Our paths collide
Imprinting on my side
Feeling so alive,
But leaving me to die

I loved you so
Very much a plateau
I thought you'd never go
But it was such a blow
When you decided to grow

I wanted you to get better
But why is it like I'm choking in my sweater

In all sunny weather
My heart can't stand the pressure

I pushed you away for a better day
But that's all up for say
All I can do is lay
In this place, we stayed
Stuck in the memories of our decay
I can't help but fray

I miss you.

Please don't leave me.
I won't deceive you.
I won't treat you like a sheet
A paper I write on and leave
When the pressure relieves
I'll come back, so, please
Don't leave.

Chapter 54

SINCE MY LAST CONFESSION

The power of impulse and quick hitting courage are powerful. So powerful that it acts before you can process the fear of the consequences.

I wrote my therapist an email one night, ready to confess to her my deepest darkest secret, and a trauma I still was trying to accept.

I. Was. Sexually. Assaulted.

I didn't have the guts and chutzpah to say it to her in person during a session, but I did have enough quick-striking courage to write her an email. I sent her this email:

Hey Doctor,

I have been writing to cope and I wanted to share this one with you. I felt that it would be important to send your way and it would be only beneficial to do so. I sure hope that I won't be let down and I sure hope that I won't regret this:

*   *   *

You've actually already read what I sent her. It was the chapter titled: Marked. Remember it? But I took the liberty of telling her that this was something I was still struggling with and this was something I still hadn't processed completely.

She responded a day later saying that she wanted to meet to discuss it and would rather not discuss it through email. At the time, we were going through a pandemic so our sessions were online. So I hopped onto the call with her that afternoon and the mood and fear began to set in.

"Hi, Wynn," her voice was of pity. *I can't hate pity.*

"Hi," I responded with a quivering smile.

"So, you sent me a kind of concerning email... and we kind of have to talk about it, okay?" *I had no choice now.*

"Okay."

"So, was it someone you know?"

"Yes."

"Someone older than you or same age or what?"

"Older."

"Are they living with you?"

"Yes."

"Okay, ummm... Wynn, I want to be entirely honest with you. But this is of a high level of concern. I am not going to push you to tell *me* who this person was, but because you are a minor, I do have to report this. I will have to send a report and a call into the Child Protective Services. Do you feel safe at home right now? Because I can tell them you don't and they can send someone to come pick you up and take you somewhere safe."

What just happened? My whole life just flashed before my eyes and I realized that my secret began to peep it's head out to the world and now is being dragged out. And along with it, the destruction that was the last straw to ruin my whole life. My family. My life. My everything.

I nodded.

"Do you have anyone in your family you trust to stay with you to keep you safe? I am obligated to make sure you are safe above all else."

"My mom."

"Is she home?"

"No."

"Would you mind calling her to come home?" *What she was asking of me was something I never wanted. I would have to tell my mother the truth. Finally. I didn't want her to find out this way. I didn't want her to find out at all.*

I called her, and she came home.

"What's wrong, honey?"

"Hi Mrs. Chau! I am sorry if I pulled you away from something important but Thành Phi just informed me of a concerning thing and I thought she needed someone to keep her safe. Thành Phi revealed to me that she had been sexually assaulted by someone in your home," she gave me a look and took a pause to show her pity and understanding for my situation. *She knew my life was falling apart in a matter of minutes.*

"I will leave you and Thành Phi to talk through things, but I will have to report this to CPS. I will write a case for Thành Phi, and I will give a call in. She said that she feels safe at home so no one will come to take her. But, CPS will contact you soon to discuss further steps."

My mother thanked her and she left the call.

And we both cried.

"What's wrong? What happened? Tell me."

"I'm sorry," *I couldn't bring myself to talk yet. My eyes were filled with tears and my heart had been shattered by the final stab of acceptance of my fate. My secret was finally out.*

She hugged me tightly in her arms like she wanted to squeeze the pain out of me, "It's okay, honey. I love you. You know that. You didn't do anything wrong. You shouldn't be sorry for anything. I love you so much. I'm sorry."

"I'm sorry," still struggling to speak, "I'm sorry this happened. I'm sorry. It's my fault. I'm sorry."

"It isn't. Listen to me. No matter what it was never your fault.

Come on now, tell mommy what happened. We can fix
anything. You and me together."

"I'm so tired, mommy."

"Was it daddy?"

I nodded, "In California last summer."

"Thành, that was over half a year ago. Why didn't you tell me? You
know I love you and I would have helped you."

"I couldn't. I just couldn't. With everything going on, I was
worried... Mommy, I was so scared."

"I know," she hugged me tighter and I felt her tears land on my
shoulder, "I know, honey. It's okay now. I love you. I
got you."

"Mommy, he touched me. Why would he do that? I shouldn't have
had to worry. I shouldn't have had to feel cautious, not
with him. He's my daddy. Why? Mommy, why did he?
I don't understand. I was so scared. I didn't know what
to do. I wanted to tell you but there were so many things
happening. I didn't know what to do."

"I know. I know. It's okay."

She hugged me and layed with me in silence until my tears stopped
pouring, and I lost all energy in me. I needed to go for a drive to get
out of my head, and my sister came home as I was leaving. My mom
told me she would tell her and she would not make me have to deal
with tiring myself out even more. I shouldn't have to do it all alone
anymore is what she said. So I left.

When I returned home, my sister aggressively, simultaneously
cried and yelled at me. She was angry I didn't tell her and she was even
more upset because the truth was that when she was little he used to
do it to her too. She just never realized when he stopped doing it to
her he did it to me. But I only remembered one time. Because I lost
all my childhood memories. They were all gone. My sister, my mom,
and I went into the room and locked the door. And we talked about
the next steps.

CPS had contacted my mother and said that soon someone

would come by to interview everyone in the home and see if the environment truly was safe for me. And then I would have to go in for an interview behind closed doors about the experience itself. The investigation would be long and grueling but permanently damaging. We all knew that. My mom and sister were a bit upset because they believed by telling CPS the truth I was ruining my dad's life for good and they didn't want to fully ruin his life. It could affect his life and he would be seen as a pedophile. He could get into some serious trouble for it. And that was true. But as much as I regretted it, I had already thought of it.

Ages ago, after the incident, my mind logically mapped out every possible scenario of how this would work. And this was the most beneficial to us all. Though it wasn't beneficial to my dad, it was the right thing to do. He was sick. He wasn't evil, just sick. Pedophelia is a sickness and you can get therapy for it, it is an urge and impulse of liking that you can get therapy and treatment for. But first you have to admit it to be true, and he hasn't. He acts normally around me. And I haven't even admitted to him that I know he did it. This was the right thing to do. I had to reassure myself as such. I had to. This process would be a long and grueling one, but it would be necessary. The investigation would take a while, but it would be worth it. I had to keep hope. I had to.

The CPS person came to our door. She interviewed my mom first. Then my sister. And finally my nanny. My dad wasn't home so they tried to call him but he didn't answer. It was my turn. I walked outside and they asked the basic questions. It's always the same ones. It was like reciting memorized answers. *Do you feel safe at home? Yes. Do you at any point feel like you might be in harm's way? Not really. Do you have a plan if something happens? Yes.*

And finally they left by telling me I will have to come in for an interview at the police station soon about it. But until then, my dad wasn't allowed to live under the same roof as me legally. Now I had to face the hardest part of this whole process. Confrontation.

"How are you going to do it?" my sister asked me in front of my mom.

"I'll just tell him to leave and don't give him a reason," my mom said.

"No." I put my foot down.

In the past, my mom has never been good at resolving or persuading my dad to listen or do anything. This is why our whole family lies have lasted so long. This is why I feel so much pain and my depression is so bad. Because my mom can't seem to figure out how to confront my dad properly, and my dad is a petty man, they talk behind each other's backs to me. This is exactly why I have so many issues. I'm done. If I want this done right, I have to take responsibility and do it myself.

"I'll do it."

"Are you sure that's a good idea? What are you going to say?" My sister was concerned.

"Mommy, you can't not give him a reason. Look at where that has taken our lives. Because of that, you are still married to him. Because of that, he is still here. And Because of that we have never had any solution, just complaining. If you do that, you'll just make him mad and we will never hear the end of it."

"Thành's right." my sister said and my mom retreated.

"I don't know yet, but it has to come from me. I know he will listen to me. He doesn't listen to anyone else." *I always was daddy's little girl.*

Though my sister and my mom felt hesitant to let me do it, they trusted me.

I sat at the kitchen table with my mom and waited for my dad to come home. My sister hid in the bedroom, stowed safe away from the storm that was about to hit.

"Hi, Thành."

"Hi, Daddy."

He sat down with his dinner and began to eat.

"I kind of need to talk to you about something."

He looked at me and knew. I knew he knew. He knew that what I was about to say was something he was already going to dislike. His face was ready for battle. I took a deep breathe and continued on.

"Mommy, is here because there is something I need to say, but she isn't going to really say anything. And what I'm about to say is going to be hard for me, so please just listen. Please just give it a chance, okay?"

"Why are you acting like this. Just say it. I won't overreact." *Lie. I spotted and anticipated that lie from a mile away.*

"So, I have depression. That's not a surprise. But do you know what one of the main reasons as to why I am depressed is? I've been depressed my whole life, but recently it's become harmful. The reason for my depression being so bad it's because I have to deal with you and Mommy's relationship."

"You don't have to deal with anything. You shouldn't have to if Mommy just talked to me or actually tried to make it work," my dad immediately began the defense and his battle started. He pointed his sword toward my mother.

"That's not the conversation I'm trying to have. I can't control her. You can't control her. And that's something we have to accept. But the thing that I can control is being honest about what it is I'm going through... Do you know I want to die every day? Do you know that you trying to hold onto this toxic relationship is why? I harm myself. I have mental breakdowns all the time. I wanna die all the time. It's because I feel responsible. I feel a burden from it all. It is tiring and it is hurting me."

"Why do you want to kill yourself, stupid? You shouldn't feel that way, it doesn't have anything to do with you..." my dad scoffed at my comments.

I quickly cut back in and stated, "It doesn't matter. It doesn't matter, none of it matters. The only thing that matters is the result. The result is that it is hurting me. Not the why, not the reason, nothing. Just it is. So I need to and beg of you to leave. Leave please. I need you and mommy to just stop. Because I'm done. I am putting my foot down. I need this. And I'm finally going to stand up for myself, because I don't care whether or not you or mommy want me to be alive, *I* don't want to die."

A long pause. My dad realized he would lose. And he accepted. He moved out. For me.

Chapter 55

THAT BUSINESS CARD

When I first came in for the first therapy session, she handed me a business card. I have been looking at it. Holding it and thinking.

Therapy is helpful for people for different reasons. It is supposed to be all around helpful and many of my friends tell me that I just need to give it time and a shot. It may just be the therapist, maybe I should get a new one. Or maybe I am not fully giving my best effort. The reality is that they have found comfort in therapy, I haven't. I am not ready to indulge in allowing someone else to tell me something I already know. I know, and I am spending the time wasting money on sitting there talking to someone about trying to get better.

Am I saying that therapy was not good for me? No. It was. Because it was how I came to resolve my problem with my family and my sexual assault all at the same time, but other than that, therapy itself hasn't done much. I appreciate the thought, but I can't seem to bring myself to talk about my issues with anyone but myself. Through writing.

So I looked at the business card. Holding it and thinking. And I stowed it away in my wallet to remember where I've been, but also ready to move on and stop therapy.

Chapter 56

NOT A VICTIM

Why are you choking me when I already can't breathe?
I am told to be strong.

But when I was in pain, no one was there to help me. When I thought it was my fault, no one reassured me it wasn't mine to selfishly take. The blame is not mine. I can't blame anyone, but I can move on.

But, apparently not.

Are you going to point a gun at me if I don't identify as heterosexual? Are you going to pull away every cent from under me because I'm a female? Are you going to diminish my flaws because I'm asian? Are you going to point a finger at me for 'asking for it'? Are you going to pick a fight with me for being alright?

I want people to stop placing me in a box.

I am not just a female. I am not just a member of the LGBTQIA+ community. I am not just a female I am not just an asian. I am not just defined by my sexual assualt. And I AM NOT a *victim*.

Every 73 seconds, an American is sexually assaulted. And every 9 minutes, that victim is a child. There are so many survivors out there. So many survivors of rape, sexual assault, sexual abuse, sexual harrassment, sexual violence and other violations of our bodies. You can look at many stories offered to other victims by survivors to promote a sense of gaining the control you've lost. Stories of using it to your benefit: don't let it break you, let it make you stronger, etc. But the difference between them and me is they seeked help.

The most important step, and you probably hear this over and over again, is to talk to someone. Get help. You are valid, and what happened to you is not okay. It was never and will never be okay. It can either make or break you. That is true. It is true, it will either make or break you. But it is so much more complicated than that. The process to either make it or even break you are both long and gruelling paths. Neither one is easy. And the real question that I constantly contemplate is *are you ever really healed?*

I think the real answer is no. You won't ever be fully healed, you'll just change. It changes you. Our responses to violations of ourselves are all different. Some people defend themselves by learning to turn a cold shoulder to the world. *If they can't get near you, you won't get hurt.* Others become advocates. Also known as the survivors. They stand as beacons to empower others to become stronger from it and keep on living. Some never open up about it. Some never tell anyone and will live with their trauma. Their trauma constantly quietly looming over them and unconsciously playing a key role in all of their decisions. Finally, some turn to death. Some turn to the only possible choice they can see clearly. They turn into their depressions arms and commit suicide or inflict self harm. As I did. Feeling burdened and haunted by the inability to ever find an answer to your questions. Feeling like your life can't be solved because the answer you need doesn't exist. Thinking maybe death is a good alternative than living a solutionless life. Knowing you will never heal can kill you in itself. It almost killed me. But I opened up. I opened up soon enough because I couldn't live with myself or my secret anymore. It was high time I faced it. It was high time I realized it was just as real as my depression. It was just as real as my self-harm. It was just as real as me and you. It happened. It all happened.

I am not a victim, I am a self-proclaimed survivor. It doesn't matter what others see, they may view me as a victim. But tell them to save and keep their sorries. I don't want them. I am a survivor. A survivor still struggling and still suffering from more than one damaging hit to my soul, but still a survivor.

Chapter 57

FALSE SENSE OF HOPE

I always thought it would get easier after I faced my biggest obstacle. I always had a certain level of blind hope that I could be happier if I finally faced my monsters. Maybe, just maybe I could be *'normal'* or at least help my mental health improve back to the way it was. I miss my old self, and I guess I had some irrational, blind hope that I could get her back. Back to when she was innocent and didn't worry about everything constantly; sure, she lacked a personality but she was still ignorantly blissful.

I miss her.

There is something no one warns you about or even blatantly lie to you about: you'll be forever changed and "you'll get better" is a lie. Don't get me wrong, maybe this method of comfort works for some people. Maybe, you can get 'better', but you'll never be perfectly happy ever again. Saddening, right? The number one cliché thing to say to someone who is going through a rough time is, "it'll get better". All you have to do is helplessly believe it's true; sometimes, that's all you're hanging onto. I hoped; I was a sucker for a brief second in my subconscious. I needed it, I needed something, anything, to make me feel like trying was worth it instead of dying.

Instead, I just felt empty. I had been numb before and I know the feeling all too well; but this time it was different. I felt misguided and lacked any sense of direction towards what to do next. Just like a floating ghost haunting the world till it finishes their unfinished business and allows them to reach a heavenly new state after. Not seeing a future, I just felt lost to relenting to thinking only about the things that had passed already. I questioned every decision I had made and wondered what would have happened if I had any detail different. There is a danger that comes with a false sense of hope, but that helpless feeling of positivity can be so agonizing when you know the reality.

It was just a false sense of hope.

Like a million tiny pulses palpitating in his hand, he felt the emotion in his fingertips. A constant shake and tremor in his hands has been ailing him ever since that fateful day. Something he can't control, like a million tiny ants drumming on every nerve in his hand. Feeling the tension in every tendon, he slowly pulled every finger in towards his palm and clenched his fist. Squeezing his fist, knowing full well that that doesn't change anything. He felt the shake cumulate throughout his whole fist now, and genuinely prayed and wished that when he released his fingers from it's protective fist the intensity would be gone. Freeing his fingers, his hand shook intensely. An intense trembling, tremoring, and telling that no amount of hoping, praying, or wishing would rid him of this. He will be stuck with it for the rest of his life. No matter how many times he hoped for it to stop when he opened his hand, it has never happened; he had a false sense of hope because he had nothing else to lean on.

It was just a false sense of hope.

Ding. A text came in. Dragging her hand along for the ride, her elbow pulled up towards the bedside table. Her fingertips dragging on the sheets, a pulling weight that refused to make the effort. Making it to the bedside table, her hand grazed over her phone screen and faintly grasped the texting box. Bringing it back to her face, she saw the text was from her mom. Her mom asked her if she wanted to go out and have bonding time. *No.* Unable to talk, unable to even find the motivation to get out of bed, she texted back. She texted back, "Fine, just let me take my meds first". Her therapist told her she needed to push herself to go against her natural instinct to say no. Her therapist said she had depression. She had a false sense of hope that her therapist, her meds, and going against her instincts to stay inside would rid her of depression; because she had nothing else to go on.

It was just a false sense of hope.

It was supposed to get easier. My life should have gotten better. It isn't fair, I should feel normal. You know, *normal* normal. My heart still craves and hopes for the day that I feel happier. The day where my tremors cease to exist. The day that having fun doesn't feel forced. The day that this false sense of hope doesn't feel like a false anymore.

Chapter 58

SUPPORT SYSTEM

I don't claim to be healed of my ailing. I don't claim to believe that I will ever be fully okay, but the difference between where I was and where I am now is support. A shoulder to lean on. My mind and thoughts have changed, and I'm ready to ask for help.

After my secret came out, my mindset changed. I realized that my life will take the turns that it may but I have to stand up for myself. I've learned my boundaries. The points that have broken me only showed me where I should stop. I need to care for myself. I have stopped fighting and feeling frustrated with my disorders, and have accepted I must live with it. But I don't have to live through it alone. My dad and my sister and my friends aren't always there. But my mom is. I've learned my support group and my support system, which is essential according to any therapist or psychologist you will ever meet.

I finally found it.

I *really* finally found it.

Chapter 59

MEET MYSELF

You may meet me today,
But keep in mind the one who may lay
Here with you may
Change.

I've never met the being
Before you. Seeing
Her own qualities
Taking in every commodity

Changing further
After another

Continuing to be changed
A continuous play, engaged
Where the main character learns,
Her insides churns,
A lesson changing the story line
Once again.

Everytime me meets myself
Personalities meld
A quality I learn
Changes another forlorn

Everytime me meets myself
I gain something new
Something new I'll learn soon
Changing through
I'm ready to pursue,
The next change that'll ensue
Another myself meets me.

Chapter 60

PER.IOD

How many chapters have you just flipped through? Do you remember every single one? Do you remember every single word? Do they each mean everything to you now like they did when you were reading them on the page? No.

The sad truth is that once you read all of this, you'll just flip the page, and what you read the page before becomes less important.

Let's have a hypothetical: you read this whole story in a column in the newspaper. Maybe you feel second-hand guilt, maybe you even feel helpless in wanting to help this girl that has gone through what she's gone through, maybe you feel like you want to do something to help her, and maybe you have sympathized and empathized for her and can't imagine what you would have done if you were in her place. Questioning everything for her, you really feel for her. Really linger in that feeling.

Flip the Page.

Ooooooh a coupon for that clothing store, shoe store, or even a coupon for kitchen supplies. Your feeling immediately vanished the minute you decided to flip the page. Maybe you still think about her once in a while, maybe she is a good conversation starter with your friends, but that feeling is gone. That moment you flipped the page, that story of the girl was just that, *a story.*

My life is full of blessings, and trust me if I could I would write one chapter for every single person in my life to tell them their impact on my life and their importance to me. But you wouldn't read that. The story that makes the front page is the tragedy, the story everyone gets hooked on is the story of death, loss, and devastation. And in retrospect, everyone else moves on; but when the story is your own, you have to live with it till you move on to the next phase after life and death. Everyone can easily judge you and make claims to know who you are through rumors and hearsay; but when they hear your truth, there is nothing for them to say.

You are about to flip the page. I never expected you to remember a *story* of a girl such as me; but life is full of stories and these stories get lost in time bunching up against each other, each fighting for their few minutes of fame on the forefront of people's minds. Don't let your story get lost in the pages. Live it. I never thought that I would write this. But it was about time I admitted my life is not fiction, and won't just end with a period and a 'The End'. A *story* doesn't end in a period or with a flip of a page, don't stop. before you reach the end

CPSIA information can be obtained
at www.ICGtesting.com
Printed in the USA
JSHW021316030323
38403JS00001B/14